My Successful

Failures

THE JOURNEY OF A THOUSAND STEPS

My Successful Failures

THE JOURNEY OF A THOUSAND STEPS

MR. NATHAN LOYD

CITI OF BOOKS

CITIOFBOOKS, INC.
3736 Eubank NE Suite A1
Albuquerque, NM 87111-3579
www.citiofbooks.com
Hotline: 1 (877) 389-2759
Fax: 1 (505) 930-7244

Ordering Information:
Quantity sales. Special discounts are available on quantity purchases by corporations,associations, and others. For details, contact the publisher at the address above.

Printed in the United States of America.

ISBN-13:   Hardback   978-1-962366-32-8

Library of Congress Control Number: 2023918707

TABLE OF CONTENTS

INTRODUCTION

T oday I break ground, at the start of 2018, as I share my painful
life growth experiences over my last three decades within my book,
'My Successful Failures'. Enjoy the ride on the value you will gain
from my personal growth of how to use Failure turned into Success in life.

Failure what is Failure?

Really failure is success turned over if we grow from our failures. I once
went skiing for the first time in my life many years ago. I found it very
interesting that our first lesson was about how to enjoy falling. Yes,
to enjoy the actual act of falling into the snow. Once we understood
how to fall, we were ready to start skiing. The way to fall had set our
minds on how to deal with a fall that would happen several times. The
difference was we already understood the art of how to fall. This made
skiing so much more fun.

*'The takeaway here is that learning how to deal with failures
beforehand makes life fun.'*

We will fail in life many times over and over. Learn the lesson from
failure and move forward.

I was taught how to ski in the state of Vermont, USA. A few lessons about the best ways to fall over the next day on the bunny slopes, I was ready for the bigger slops. I only got better at skiing after learning to fail through falling. We tend to think that failing is the end, yet it is the beginning.

'Failure is actually a beautiful covering of success'

It's only by failing and learning the lesson that we grow. This means each time you fail, you learn that lesson and grow from the experience. Once you learn the specific lesson, you will have grown and understood how not to handle the same in the future.

'As the outside world, especially the critics, discuss your failures, you know in your heart you have succeeded through failure'.

Now both words, Fear and Failure, start with "F." In the alphabet, after the letter "F" comes "G," which is the first letter in the word Growth. We change our "F" for Fear into our "G" for Growth which brings the next letter in the alphabet, which leads to "H." The first letter in the word Health. We cannot grow without failure. The more you fail and learn the lesson, the more you grow.

"Always remember the solution is Always within the Problem."

We tend to shy away from problems, yet the very solution is within the very same problem'

'Dog Senses'

When we look at a dog, for example, it has a greater sense of smell than we do. On the business side, our senses are only heightened through having tried and failed and learned the lesson. Our business sense is heightened through learning valuable lessons. I strongly believe that the more times one has failed, the more success is gained through growth.

'One has only failed if one allows the past to hold them back'.

Therefore, learn from the experience, and enjoy the past experiences, for this is where you will find true growth.

The biggest issue I see from my point of view is letting fear paralyze you.

'Our Success roots are based on failing, and each time we fail, we grow new and deeper roots.'

The deeper the roots, the stronger and better to support our growth. I must say over the years, I have failed and bounced back and failed again and come back better and sharper.

Over the years, I have seen close friends, family and different people I know never grow. One of the reasons is that they never try. This group lives their lives mainly watching and criticizing others' failures. If you are getting criticized, take heart as it is because you are making a difference in this world. I tell you that those critics are not getting criticized because they are doing nothing positive in this world. Friends always smile from within when family members criticize you because you are making a difference! It's amplified even more in one's "failure" through the positive impact one has in this world of ours.

'When we learn from our Failures, we will become better and not bitter'.

Thought Builders note to Self:

"There will be No change if One does Not Change."

"The true beauty of Mental, Spiritual, and Soul-searching growth comes through one's amazing Failures."

"In every failure, there is a message. Some people miss the message by concentrating too much on the mistake. Reflect on that failure and learn from it!"

Successful Failures Lesson Take Away:

Come let's go, join me on the journey of your lifetime, with true insights on how to turn failure upside down to totally change your life forever.

'As we Fail, we Grow. That's the secret to true success. We need to become Great at "Successfully Failing.'

CHAPTER: 1 – 'MASTERS OF DECEPTION'

Description: 'The Land of a thousand Lies.'

'Silence Broken Twelve Years On'

My silence is broken after twelve years to give the other true side of what really happened in Rwanda.

'I kept silent to stay alive from my tormentors and not tell my side of the story on what really happened.'

Now finally twelve years later you get to read all about the horror of what really happened for the very first time, here in my book in 2023.

'The Tiger'

I lived and worked in Rwanda through my thirties from 1999 to 2011.

During my years in Rwanda, I was a key top player, in support of building a nation that had just come out of the ashes. I started my construction business from zero in 2003 with not even a single coin. I had the willpower and the drive to push forward each day.

My first involvement was in the minerals trading business for just over three years. We traded in different minerals mainly from Congo and exported the minerals to Europe.

That was a perfect time to start my construction business since Rwanda had just come out of a terrible genocide. Rwanda was in urgent need of rebuilding its infrastructure, and my new DN International was ready and in place at the right time. My company grew at a very fast rate to become one of the top five leading Construction/Developers companies.

'I was known as the Tycoon upcoming Tiger"

My wealth grew as I became a millionaire in dollars by my mid thirties. I can tell you what grew with my riches was my arrogance and pride. I enjoyed using the word 'SelfMade' because I thought and felt I was 'SelfMade.' This word 'Self-made' fed my growing ego to make it appear that I did this alone.

'Building a Nation.'

At the peak of my construction company DN international I had several projects under construction and we also doubled up as a developer. We had grown to a huge team of over 400 workers to include all our projects on the ground. The value of our projects had grown to over Seven million dollars in 2009.

Additionally, I was putting together a mega housing project, set to break ground in 2010, of over Seventy-Five million dollars. This was to develop a full mini city with housing units, schools, a shopping center and a church within a sweet piece of land I bought. The eight-five acres of land I bought was nested only about seven kilometers from town down Kigali. This was prime land, which I bought out of my boldness to support the building of a nation, Rwanda.

My boldness was mixed with my passion to support in building my new home in this tiny nation, Rwanda.

'Punitive Law cracks started.'

The shift in the mortgage law came into place. The cause and start of the downfall of the empire I had built checked in with the new punitive mortgage law.

'Mr Nathan Questions President Paul Kagame.'

During a round time meeting in the year 2010, I was able to question Kagame if he was aware of the damage he has caused through signing this ridiculous law into place.

I had every right to ask the question as this mortgage law shift brought down a giant, DN International, to an ant within twelve months.

'Focus on the Cause to know the Real Truth.'

The cracks started to show as Rwanda's legislative government shifted the mortgage law. A shift in the Rwandan mortgage law to counter the USA real estate sector bubble burst of 2019 the Rwandan government acted with a knee-jerk reaction. The two showstoppers had been one; the mortgage law shifted from 30% down payment & 70% bank financing to vice versa 70% over 30%. This means the home buyer is required to put a down payment of 70% cash and get the balance of 30% funds from one's bank.

Two, it gets worse with this new ridiculous mortgage law. In the event of default, the bank is not allowed to foreclose on the financed property. The homeowner would have to issue a letter of consent to allow the bank to foreclose and take back the house.

'Understand this to know the Cause.'

Let's look at the cause, not just the effects, to always understand the core of any issue or challenge. Focus needs to be on the cause. When the US faced the mortgage real estate issue back in 2009, that led to the bubble bust. The US government faced the issue at hand as difficult as it was and made the needed changes to start bouncing back for the good of its US Citizens.

At just around this time the Rwandan government passed a punitive legislative shift in the mortgage law in 2010. So now the original Mortgage law was 30% deposit from the buyer and 70% from bank financing; this was switched to vice versa. The challenge was made even worse with all the banks in Rwanda folding their arms refusing to issue any mortgage loan countrywide. This stemmed from the fact that the law also stated in the event that the buyer might go into default on his/her loan payments to the bank. The buyer will have to give the bank written consent to allow the bank to take over the said property. This means if you go into default for whatever reason after borrowing funds from the bank. One still has the power to decide if you allow the bank to take your property. Towards the end of 2011, it was just too late for me since my life was already threatened, and I was on the run for my life. At the close of 2011, the Rwandan Government saw fit to play the victim and turn the tables around to claim I cornered a few people of their properties.

'They mixed up the lies to cover up the cause and show the effects of hunting me down as a method to correct their own wrong.'

The art of deception continued as the Rwandan authorities placed me on Interpol. Yes, on Interpol to hunt me down with the aim of finding me, to silence me. In Rwanda, there is one best way; they silence anyone who has made a mistake or might give an objective option. Lock you up, and within a very short time, something happens, and you disappear off the face of this earth forever. The level of secrets and lies have worked to benefit Rwanda as donors continue to be fooled going back over the last thirty years.

'The donors have been successfully fooled to pump in billions of Dollars over the last thirty years.'

This punitive law shifted my life upside down as the cracks grew deeper in 2010 and crossed to 2011. Let's also know that this crazy, punitive law lasted for just shy of two years, into 2012. This shifted everything, my business, my family, down to nothing, to zero! My Rwandese wife,

Cleophase Kabasiita, fled to the USA, my second home with my son Darrel and daughter Crystal.

'It's from the USA, my American home that Cleophase now focused to become my biggest critic.'

I, on the other hand, fled to Kenya back to my birth home country.

'Let's take a deep breath & hold for five seconds'

Now, this is where the story started to turn, and the false claims started that I was personally taking depositors funds. This is for those who had put down payments of 30% and had been unable to raise the 40% to reach the new down payment of 70%. In addition other potential home buyers with provisional sales purchase agreements had been unable to raise the difference of funds. In provisional sales agreement, one clause covered, in the event of default the deposit is forfeited & the said house reverts back to the developer. Once a house is legally back to the developer, the developer is free to re-sell the same house on the open market. Now get this the Rwanda Authorities charged me with a crime of selling the same house twice. Yes, you guessed it the very same house that went into default & the said person lost their house.

'Keep in Mind this.'

Keeping in mind that we had ordered building materials from China and other countries that arrived with my projects at a standstill. No sales for months means no income for months on one end.

'I was then arrested and jailed for 14 days and released with no charges at all, Zero'

The threats started as I also faced numerous cases in court due to non-payment of our suppliers. I had no option but to flee for my life. The country I had given my eleven years to and had fallen in love with showed its true colors as the devil within.

'Rwandan authorities jumped in to do what they do best, point the finger at someone else.'

It made it simpler for them to pass the blame over to me with the finger now pointed at me. The focus was on the effects, not the cause of the punitive law that Kagame had signed into place.

'CEO to Fugitive'

I was now called a fugitive, claiming I sold one house twice with a list of other lies. The aim and what they are good at is to never admit a mistake and pass the blame onto the other party.

'Then, Rwanda does what it does best, to play the victim.'

The same group, same friends, and same high officials turned their backs on me. My once close friends on all levels became my foes. I was on the run for my life, with threats to clear me off this earth with no trace of finding my body.

'Be Warned'

In Rwanda, once you get threatened, you must take it very seriously. I took the threats on my life for real and worked to keep as much distance between myself and Rwanda as possible to avoid its evil deeds. Rwandese have picked up the art of showing the world the clean side, the proper side. It's all about whether the image is real or not; they will still make you think and feel like they are perfect.

'The problem is not them in any way; the issue is you. '

The few brave enough to try and shed light on these issues, or any issues, disappear off this earth. The locals live in full fear and trauma and are unable to even dare try and give their opinion. These poor people live day and night in never-ending torture. I find this life a sorry state of fake living, a very sad state and way to live.

In Rwanda one's only focus is to keep silent and agree to everything said by Paul Kagame.

'I acted on the bravest option and fled for my life in October 2011. I live today as I write my first book due to my bravery and turning to God as my shield'. This has grown me into a better-refined man with Scars on my back that have turned into Stars.

The Art of the Lying Truth.

My great escape from a land few get to know the truth about, a tiny country called Rwanda. This country is filled with mystical secrets that are hidden from the rest of the world.

'Mistake Is a Crime.'

This little small country, where a mistake is and can be turned into a crime, is called Rwanda. Make a mistake, in my case, a so-called business mistake, in a matter of days; the Rwandan authorities will do what they do best, arrest you and cover up the truth.

Take a pause; the oversight mistake was caused by the very same authorities. However, their aim is to turn this around and play the victim as they continue to finger-point to avert any responsibility. The image to the world at large is to show perfection at the expense of thousands of tears, and thousands of blood drops shed as thousands go missing.

'Fake Hero'

The pretense comes from the very top in Rwanda, the President of Rwanda Paul Kagame. This gives him an overall feel of always playing and being seen as the Hero. This feeds his ego more and more as the lie is believed over and over. The lie has been perfected in a way that the world at large, for the most, believes to be true.

'Think Different Bye Bye'

In Rwanda, do not even try to think differently or show any sign that you do not agree with Kagame's government.

'The true poor leadership skills of the president, alongside his fear, are shown through his dictatorship.'

My so-called mistake turned into a crime was the mortgage law shift. The new unfriendly business environment brought my company to its knees within twelve months of this law that blocked the selling of our houses. Then Rwanda's governmental authorities kicked in and created fake news as they do best.

'Master Cover Ups'

Rwandese have become so good at covering up the truth over the last twenty-five years. They have managed to paint a country for the international community to see for the sake of donor funds. It is through this false image and false economy that Rwanda survives on.

Friends, do not think, look or breathe in a manner that might show that you do not agree with President Kagame. If you dare try, in a matter of days, the story about you starts to change, and you become the problem due to the difference of opinion. Once you become the problem, you will face numerous other problems, and your life will be at risk.

This has given birth to the false image that Rwanda is tough on corruption.

How sad that no one is able to try and call out the human rights abuses that take place every day in Rwanda.

'I wonder if the image is not the reality and if the growth numbers are not a reality. Who is really the corrupt one at the end of the day?'

I too was a victim, as they turned a civil offense into a criminal offense, and I was labeled a conman.

Friends, it gets worse if you dare to try and give your side of your story. All options are deployed on the table to include your disappearance from this earth. Be Warned.

'The dictatorship leadership style used by Paul Kagame is one to never be even questioned. Those who have tried too have cried alone and disappeared into the night.'

'I am the only American Survivor to have Survived Paul Kagame by God's Grace.'

'This is one of the great acts of deception Rwandese Authorities have perfected the art of lying turned into false truths. Then they cry wolf & pretend they are going after the corrupt with false accusations.

'Makes me ponder how the corrupt call the innocent corrupt.'

'This starts from the very top President Paul Kagame is the Master of deception.'

Making him the most corrupt President in Africa yet kept as a continued cover up.

'My Crossing Point'

I have had many dark nights, long days with tears filled heartaches over the long last twelve years. My days, My weeks, My months and years of insults of being called names to reflect the opposite of who I am. I was on the run from October 2011 from a very deceitful country that had one mission to cover up the real truth to look better and feel better for themselves. I had to escape and save my life from Rwanda, the place I called home for eleven years.

'My foes' aim was to silence me at any cost, should I dare give my side of the story.'

I was in hiding, on the run for my life. My former Rwandese Wife Cleophase Kabasiita decided to call it quits in my darkest days. My Dad's health started to fail due to complications from diabetes.

I watched sadly my father, during the last three years of his life, turn into a very bitter man. He was angry at the mistakes he had made in the past and did not learn from his failures. This added to his failing health. We checked into 2012, my Dad passed on, and the Rwandan authorities pressed on to find me with the overall aim of making sure I kept silent through their threats.

'There I was, beaten, bewildered on my knees shaking in total shock that my life had come to this. I asked myself, is this how my life will end? '

Rwandan authorities' overall aim was to discredit me and embarrass me and humiliate me on false charges. This gives them the justification to have free will to do as they please. They increased the hurt by placing me on Interpol in February 2012. The aim was for a search to find and destroy. The extent of this whole ordeal had a key missing link.

What was the cause and who was the tiger ?

Who caused the cause?

'Rwanda has taken the path of being a deceitful country for self-gain for donor funds at the stake of millions of lives left to suffer under an oppressive regime ruled by the dictator President Paul Kagame.'

'Smile of Scars Turned into Stars.'

As I look back at my last seven years towards the end of 2018, I am in joy, delight, and in peaceful shock. It was after seven long years, I was finally able to travel again. Keeping in mind one of the methods the Rwandan authorities used to try and capture me was placing me on 'INTERPOL' as a most wanted man. I was placed on the same list as genocide suspects for a civil debt turned criminal. Rwandese have trained minds to lie at any cost to cover up the truth.

IF YOU WANT TO BE SUCCESSFUL, FACE YOUR FEARS BECAUSE A KING IS NOT BORN, HE IS MADE. WORK HARD

'This is done to perfection with cover-up after cover-up. The aim is they need to look good to the world at large.'

After seven long years, unable to do my business and travel as an entrepreneur to meet my international clients. I was finally able to board a plane for Europe. I was free like a bird, free to spread my wings again. I did not bribe anyone to get my freedom.

'I turned my love and attention to God. I did the part I was able to handle and gave God His part to handle as my maker, my creator.'

We must have both Prayer and action. Too many times, I see so much Prayer from friends and family but on actions behind one's prayers. Our Prayers and Actions Must go hand in hand. This is part of the main reason God has gifted us to do our parts and use our gifts also.

As in our Word, Our Bible, *'No weapon fashioned against me will prosper....'* I have seen and felt God's hand in my life. I have felt His peaceful whisper say, **"Nathan, I am with you."** These seven years, by 2018, have been a battle as old friends took off. I now know those old friends that took off; looking back had never really been my friends at all in the first place.

Letting go has not been easy. Watching my ex-wife turn her back on me was Not Easy. Watching my kids leave me was Not easy. Watching as I was pulled into court was Not Easy. Watching as the Rwandan authorities hunted me down was Not Easy. Watching and listening to what the press claimed I did and called me a con-man was Not Easy. Watching former close friends point fingers at my downfall with joy was Not Easy. Watching as the Lord said to me to be patient was Not Easy.

'Cause and effects'

In life, we often forget the causes and focus on the effects. It's the causes that point to and lead to the effects, not the other way around. Yet, funny enough, we are quick to pass judgment with words like did you hear this or that.

'This is how rumors get started, as the focus is on the effects.'

It is vital to always take time to reflect and focus on the cause. This is one of the main reasons judges delay passing final judgments without fully understanding the root causes. The causes give birth to the effects.

In my case, when I fled from Rwanda, all focus was on the effects. He is a liar, he is a thief, he is a conman, and he has taken people's money. The focus is on the effects. Yes, I ran away for my life due to the threats on my life and the fact that one cannot get a fair trial in Rwanda. This is a country that has and continues to hide its truth and true nature. It is only in these later days that I have come to see how brave I was.

'Sometimes in life, it is very brave to run away'.

So, What was the cause and who was the tiger ?

'The cause was the punitive mortgage law signed in place and the tiger has always been my Ex-Wife Cleophase Kabasiita.'

Who caused the cause?

'Legislative law signed into law by President Paul Kagame was the cause. Now Kagame should come out clean.

'The spin of showing Rwanda as a success story under Kagame has worked for Kagame as he plays the victim. It's through the level of playing the victim that the President wants to be looked at as a hero. It's through the victim's nature that he has and continues to commit international crimes against humanity. It is just not possible to have any success story at the stake of human rights violations. At stake, billions of liters of blood secretly spilled.'

Please visit:
https://www.theguardian.com/world/2023/oct/10/rwanda-accused-of-broad-campaign-of-repression-against-dissidents?fbclid=IwAR3qeni0 KYAZeKfaYI56ixo7LDw4gCwW6wo0MY aXziC7j5kiHRSKYASJg aem AW92KsEovuPPEedBU8d4 4IFZKZwIeSfu8KzEFxU1YVHvNt 7AOXw2tK9R5DP0C-7D1s&mibextid=2JQ9oc

'At Core'

At the core is the brave action of pulling away to change the ending of my chapter in Rwanda. The true cause was the mortgage law shift brought me & my company to its knees. Then this very deceitful nation Rwanda goes after thousands of people with the focus on the effects. Keeping in mind the cause was an oversight on their part, signed into law by Kagame, that has never been admitted.

'President Paul Kagame is simply a coward pretending to be a Hero, a fake Hero.

'Blow up Again Coming Soon'

Let's remember nothing in life happens all of a sudden at all. Let's look at a volcano. It takes years of building pressure before the blow-up. In the same manner, a steam cooker will take a few minutes before you get to hear it blow steam. This is my view of the current political climate in which no steam is allowed out but is building up year after year. The next blow up is coming to Rwanda very soon.

'Thoughts to Self:'

'As I look back on my adult life today, I am amazed, pleased, and in joy. As I went through the fire and the finger-pointing of evil people, I now smile with the joy of overcoming them all. This only took place by God's grace, even if I did not know it then'.

'I acted on the bravest option and fled for my life in October 2011. I live today as I write my first book due to my bravery and turning to God as my shield'.

This has grown me into a better-refined man with Scars on my back that have turned into Stars.

'Huge Skeletons'

Friends, for the most part, Rwandese are brainwashed to protect and hide the truth. This country has huge skeletons hidden successfully for now. One key task is to cover up the causes and focus on the effects only. The Rwandan authorities have perfected the underlying issues into an art of lies. The focus remains on the "effects," for this justifies their means of human rights violations. This makes them look good to the world at large, heavily dependent on foreign aid.

Please visit:

https://www.cnn.com/2022/07/26/africa/us-rwanda-human-rights-intl

'Friends, sometimes the true hero must keep silent and watch with a smile as others focus on the effects. The truth is starting to come Out to shed light on the true Hero I became'

I thank God I am back safely home on My American Soil, miles away from my tormentors.

Successful Failures Lesson Take Away:

The hunt continues to find me since 2011. This is over twelve years on with the aim of how to silence me by any means necessary. I do really mean any means necessary. Friends, take time to do your homework on any country you want to invest in and listen to those who have gone before you.

Chapter 2 - The Great Escape

The Great Escape.

The runaway, the dark day, the drizzling cold rain, and the cold hearts of my former friends turned into foes and started hunting me down.

I remember the feeling of a shock wave directly through my heart mixed with bewildering thoughts.

It was a dark afternoon with raindrops on my back and I was on the back of a public motorbike, fleeing for my life towards the Uganda border.

I was on the run as I sat at the back of this public motorbike, on the run from what had become my second home, Rwanda. My thoughts streamed in; after 11 years, is this how my life will end? After all the years of hard work rebuilding Rwanda up Post genocide.

Imagine this, in a matter of days; I went from being a pioneer CEO of a major company to being on the run for my life. Over these eleven years I was one of the biggest positive change makers in making Rwanda a better, more comfortable place to live in. I did improve the lives of thousands of people for the better in Rwanda.

'Cunning Foes.'

My heart pumped faster and harder. I thought about how tactful and cunning my new foes who created the problem were and passed the blame over to me to carry the cross. I must say, the stage was set, and the run to the Uganda border was in high gear through the ghostly fields. I looked up at the dark clouds on my bumpy ride and felt empty. My heart was shattered, and time stopped as I was on the run but in a dazed glaze. Everything is finished!

In a glass eyed gaze with my eyes filled with tears, I thought about how I had flown into Rwanda over eleven years ago. Now I was on the run escaping on a public motorbike for dear life. I was with my former Kenyan high school friend called Edwin Muturi as we dashed across the Rwandan hills heading out of Rwanda. We crossed through different farmlands into the bushes and over a slipper tree log & over a raging river.

I was leaving all my earthly riches, my family, and my home totally destroyed. I was done; I was finished as I thought; I was broken, shattered into a thousand pieces.

Keeping in mind, my foes would never expect that I would dare to escape through the woods. As a high-profile businessman, they would expect me to try and leave the country through the airport. The moment came as I came off the public Motorbike and started my dangerous crossing over the slippery log.

I walked across and onto Uganda soil. As my shaking feet touched Uganda's soil, I looked over to Rwanda with a deep sigh of relief.

'My emotions exploded with Joy, Fear, Sadness, and Shock!'

I asked myself, "Nathan, is this really happening to you? Are you on the run?" I was talking to myself like a mad man, for I was in shock, and the shock waves just kept coming.

Once across the river that separated me from my new tormentors.

'I looked back at Rwanda for the last time in shocking disbelief; after eleven years, I was on the run for my life.'

Yet, on the run not due to a so called business mistake but for a clean over up, to cover their mistake.

The Great Escape continues Part 2.

My escape continued deeper into Uganda. I used public transport for the first time in my adult life. My aim was to place as much distance between Rwanda as possible. I needed to get further and further away, knowing that even the Uganda border shared the same soil as the Rwandan border soil. This fact alone made me feel very uneasy.

I pressed on for Kenya, my home, without a single identification document as I walked into no man's land, the official border between Uganda and Kenya. My knees were weak from Fear as I looked across and saw a beautiful flag.

'The flag blowing in the wind was the flag of My birth home, My country, My Kenya.'

My heart raced with each step as I pretended to talk with strangers to avoid any questions from the authorities. If the authorities stopped me and asked where is your passport. I would be cooked and held in jail to be questioned on my lack of having my passport. This I wanted to avoid at all costs and act as naturally as possible. Imagine acting as naturally as possible as your killers are trying to find out where you are to eliminate you.

Then it happened!!

My feet touched Kenyan soil. I found the first kiosk and ordered chips and a soda as I gazed with joy, Karibu Kenya! I was back home, thousands of miles away from my tormentors. '

'I was just gazing & in confused shock. I took a huge deep breath as I held back my tears.'

I am Home. I survived this first part of my ordeal. My steps continued with the remembrance that I was on the run from an issue created by the Rwandan authorities.

'Then turned around to point the finger at me as Rwanda played what it does best. They play the victim to justify the cause.

I was a fugitive on the run for my life. It's so strange when I look back at a non-issue taking center stage.

Touch Down !!

I touched down in Nairobi after over one thousand five hundred kilometers and after five days of being on the run from my former home country Rwanda into my birth country Kenya. I drove into my apartment in Hurlingham, where dad and my eldest brother Ben lived and, from time to time, my younger half-brother. They welcomed me, a brand-new fugitive on the run for my life from Rwandan authorities.

'I knew the hunt was on from the Rwandan side with a clear mission to silence me and destroy me.'

On my end, the crossing point, with a new bewildered look, trying to grasp what just happened. Let me make this picture clearer in focus. In five days, I had gone from the CEO of one of the very top real estate companies to a fugitive. The stories hit the headlines, I was placed onto "Interpol," and the hunt to have me killed was on.

'The rumors blared on, and the Rwandan authorities did what they do best: lie and play the victim. The role of playing victim justifies the reason for hunting me down like a genocide suspect.'

Lost on the inside:

There I was, totally lost on the inside but acting like all was in control on the outside. There I was with an ailing father. There I was as my former Rwandese Wife Cleophase took to the heels and took my kids away with her. There I was as she turned her back on her husband and joined the critics in pointing fingers at me. There I was, as the second born, handling the role of the firstborn & my fathers failing health. There I was in the worst financial mess of all my siblings, yet I still had to carry the weight of supporting my father. There I was, a visitor in my own home in Hurlingham as I had to give my dad the Master Bedroom. There I was to handle everything else when my life was upside down. There I was, full of tears of pain as I cried myself to bed almost every night in total bewilderment.

My heart was broken into a thousand pieces, and my life was empty. The pain deep down in my chest felt like I could not even breathe some nights. I watched in shock as my friends and family turned their backs on me and believed the lies coming out of Rwanda as truths. My Rwandese wife Cleophase joined the critics on the side of my foes.

"When The Heart Bleeds."

It is really sad how many family members and friends come to the aid to support your distraction. In and during 2011 and 2012, my physical world blew up; my business was destroyed, and my now ex-wife Cleophase Kabasiita turned on me. My two kids were taken away by her to the USA. It was during these lost moments of mine I would reach out to my wife then and seek her support.

'It broke my heart as she distanced herself from me several times and gave me the cold shoulder.'

In fact, her response had been, 'I told you so.' She enjoyed the pain I felt, and this hurt me to the core. This was the same lady I Loved and said I do too in Marriage.

'I was so bewildered and in shock for months on end at how cold Cleophase had become.'

My heart bled with shock for months on end. My little boy Darrel and Little girl Crystal did come back to start living with Daddy in the year

2013. This turned into a legal battle with my ex-wife in 2014 as she dragged me into the Kenyan courts for custody of our kids. This is a story for another day.

Let's keep in mind I was a fugitive on the run from my tormentors. On the run from a country, I called home for eleven years, Rwanda.

'I was placed on the Interpol list of the top 10 most wanted people alongside genocide suspects.'

The threats and the hunt for me continued with the aim of silencing me. The aim was to make sure I should never try and give my side of the story. As Rwanda will go to all lengths on the table to make sure the other side is omitted by omitting me as their aim.

'Rwandese authorities have this perfected to keep an image at all costs, even if built on lies.'

I also turned to seek advice from my brother-in-law Aziz and close friend then George Rabala. I opened my heart to them to ask for their advice. Do I keep my kids or send them back to their mother in the USA? Here are the responses I got:

"Let them go; you are in big trouble. It is also best that you go into hiding up-country; why fight when you are destroyed? Have you done a 'Google Search' on your name? It is terrible!"

These two gentlemen pushed to pump me up with fear upon fear. The ill advice continued as they both said my life would be simpler without having to take care of my kids. These two men are married with kids, offering me advice, yet they would do the opposite if they were in my shoes. The same two men would go home at night to their wives and kids and go to bed with smiles on their faces. Keep this in mind these same two men face far reaching challenges of their own. Plus, have far less ownership of their own fatherly roles.

In the coming days, weeks, and months, my empty heart felt like my blood was bleeding out. During special moments I would look deep into my Son and Daughters' eyes to give them a Father's comfort. My Soul echoed, "I am your Father, and I will continue the fight until my last breath."

'My Father in Heaven stands with me, and I am with Him, Forever.'

Over the coming weeks, my fear switched to faith! My relationship blossomed with my kids, and we continued to grow up together with God at our center. As I was growing in my faith, so did my kids, as we became members of Nairobi Chapel Church. I pulled back from getting advice from the wrong people, family, and friends. I focused on my relationship with God and got in touch with my Soul daily.

As I look back, I remember these dark nights; what stood out was God, whom I should have sought advice from. I should have turned my focus deeper on God.

Over the coming years, I started to seek God's advice more and more. Yes, I fought forward with God's strength within me and brought up my wonderful Son and Daughter, who are now both young adults. The messages of love from Darrel and Crystal as young adults fill Dad's heart to know that through the dark nights, I made the best decision and fought for my kids.

'As my Father in Heaven fights for me, I fight for my kids, as their Father here on earth.'

During the year 2018, my two kids, almost young adults in 2018, left for the USA for further studies. As I had done the same two decades ago, with also solid African Christian values.

'I am in total peace with joy, knowing even as my heart bleeds to be a father, I was a father.'

This pride and joy were never robbed from me, and this is one of my greatest victories and successes. This was a long, painful lesson over seven years, but it turned out beyond perfect.

'This was yet another successful failure, another feather in my hat, as I learned the value of turning to God and turning fear into faith.'

In addition, it built my faith on the Rock, Jesus Christ, my Rock!

"Power Of Unknown Love."

During special occasions, we would travel upcountry to spend the day with my grandmother from my Father's side. My grandmother was a very strong believer and a Prayer Warrior. I would listen to her powerful voice as she Prayed. At least twice a year, when I lived in Rwanda, I would travel upcountry to meet Cucu/Grandmother.

'I remember my thoughts so vividly when she Prayed for me to be covered with the blood of Jesus Christ in Rwanda.'

Her Prayer was a Prayer of protection over me. On my end, I would open my eyes wide in shock for I would look at her and think in my mind why ? My Grandmother from my fathers side, really does not know who I am. I am in my thirties; I am strong, I am rich, and powerful.

Does 'Cucu' my Grandmother know who I am? I am a millionaire in dollars many times over. I am untouchable and on one-on-one bases with the President of Rwanda. I am on the who-is-who list, and I got this.

'I felt like superman, strong and untouchable and able to do anything to anyone as I please.'

I had cars to match my clothes and did not want anyone to even dare try and advise me. My shoes used to be taken off by the househelp when I got home in Rwanda. I enjoyed it as people around me cheered me on, and this fed my ego more and more.

'Womanizing and alcoholism formed my weekly life throughout my thirties.'

I felt and acted like I was on top of the world. Please don't get me wrong; I enjoyed that lifestyle. As my ego grew, my pride grew bigger and bigger. Little did I know my world and life in Rwanda were about to come tumbling down at the turn of the year 2011.

I thought: 'Why would I need protection in Rwanda?' I know the top person and have enough money to protect myself all through. Little did I know, 'Silly Me', in a few short years my world in Rwanda would blow up.

The cracks with steam coming up started to show, just after I turned thirty nine years old. The blow up of hot lava blast into the air took place just after I turned forty years old.

My life in Rwanda had come to an end; it was over, and I was on the run for my dear life. The voice that echoed in my heart and mind was my Grandmother's voice. It was at this time I knew crystal clear what she meant, ***"May the blood of Jesus Christ Protect you, Nathan."*** The words in Psalm 18 especially would become so true in my heart over the coming months & years.

> *"You gave me victory*
>
> *Over my accusers*
>
> *You hold and held me*
>
> *Safe beyond the reach*
>
> *Of my enemies."*

When I thought I was it and had it all, I was dead wrong! Friends, the people, and the country I called home for eleven years turned to foes. I was hunted down by Rwandese authorities in the same manner as hunting a wild animal.

'The aim was never about the truth, but the focus has always been how to silence me, Kill me'

It's been over fifteen years since my grandmother went to be with the Lord. However, her message feels like it was fifteen minutes ago.

Cucu's message: *'in my Heart was Jesus who loved you yesterday, loves you today, and will love you tomorrow.'*

I was surprised that God Loved me when I had a long-distance relationship with him, during my thirties especially. I did not really know God in my thirties, and neither did I have much time for Him. This was shocking to me for God to still Love me when I really did not Love Him.

'I now know the true meaning of unconditional love, God's love for me.'

'Salue Dad.'

As I look back at my life experiences, I marvel at all my growth from failed experiences. I feel blessed and deeply proud of all the value-added experiences along this journey called life. My dad was a very hardworking businessman and very aggressive, and I learned a lot from him.

'I owe a great deal to my father for taking the bull by its horns and going after one's dreams. In this part I have followed in his footsteps'

My venture into Rwanda came about from his invitation for me to join him in doing mineral business in Rwanda. *I salute you, Dad.*

Sadly, I watched my dad, over the last ten years of his life, filled with anger and bitterness, take center stage in his life. He was angry at the mistakes in his life that he made and could not change. This bitterness gets under one's skin and starts to kill one slowly.

'We cannot and are not able to change our pasts, but we can change our futures. **We can change our tomorrows through learning from our yesterdays.'**

A key lesson I learned was the value of failed experiences turning us from bitter to better. It is truly soul-soothing and refreshing to grow from failed experiences. It gets even better when one grows and laughs about one's experiences. When we grow and learn, we fail forward. We only fall downwards, called downfall, if we do not get up. I must say, I have learned to fail upwards, not downwards. This is because I take time to learn from my valuable experiences and failures that have built me up over the years.

'The word'

The Lord has heard my plea; the Lord will answer my prayers.

May all my enemies be disgraced and terrified.

May they suddenly turn back in shame.

Psalm 6:9-10

He reached down from heaven and rescued me;

He drew me out of deep waters.

Psalm 18:16

<u>Thought to Self:</u>

"I did; I achieved touch down with tears of joy streaming down my face as I reflect on my successful failures through my thirties into my forties and victory touch down at the start of my fifties! "

> 'Our yesterdays are to be used to build us, not destroy us.'

> Always check and ask yourself, who should I get advice from?

> Seek God above all else.

> Learn the bitter hard lesson and grow from the experience.

> I have grown from these painful experiences to become a valuable mentor.

> Google search is not who I am; focus on God search is all you need.

Successful Failures Lesson Take Away:

True courage.

A surprising fact we might not know is that those who try and fail are very courageous. We sometimes hear those on the sidelines saying, "I would not have done that," or "I would have planned things better and done better." Those weak minds trying to look courageous from the sidelines do not add value. The doers of this world are the courageous ones; we make a difference in this world and leave this world a Better Place.

Chapter 3 - Simplicity

Description: Thought Builders.

We think life is hard, difficult, and impossible, yet life's key secrets lie in simplicity. *One key secret is balance.* We have time for everything, but we just make it look like we are always out of time!

Take time, QT "quiet time" every day, or at least five days a week. It does not need much time, maybe thirty minutes to hear, connect, reflect or enjoy 'you.'

'Yes! You need to enjoy spending time with yourself.'

As you enjoy these simple, powerful moments, your heart grows in peace. God's Word, the Bible, says many times over, "may peace be with you" Jesus valued His QT moments as He pulled Himself away from the crowds. During these moments, you grow in peace, thoughts, and love.

Ladies take time every morning to beautify their faces, sometimes for up to thirty minutes. We all need to take time to beautify our hearts. This can only be done through balance and having your QT time. Fall in love with yourself first so you can understand who you are and love others.

'When we say, "I wish I had more time," it only means I wish I had balanced my time better.'

We have time for everything, but we might be spending too much time in only one area. Keep in mind that whatever we focus on grows. This is across all sectors: mind, body, and soul. Our minds grow like every other muscle when we feed it with positive growth thoughts. Our bodies grow when we train and build up our muscles, and our spirit grows when we build up our spiritual muscles.

'My loved ones, it is simple; it is all about balance.'

Keep it simple; let's continue to grow like children. In the Bible, Jesus says these children will enter the Kingdom of heaven. Why??? ***Keeping it simple with love.*** So many times, as adults, we stop growing because we have blocked our growth with too many complications. We need to take one step at a time with balance and simplicity.

I think and wonder how come we live a life full of curiosity and failure and do not grow. It is simple in the middle of it all; we focus all our energy on what went wrong. In turn, we move our focus from getting better to only becoming bitter.

"We need to learn from these greatest lessons called experience."

When we learn, we grow. The point is that we have total control over our reactions. As the saying goes, ten percent is what happens to us, and 90 percent is our reaction.

'Passion must have action. Passion fuels the fire, which gives us determination, and actions give us the force, the direction.'

'Planning with Action'.

I joined a powerful book club called "3 to 5" in November 2014. I have finished reading the current book we are studying; the title is "Is Making money killing your business." We will talk more about the growth and the system factors gained. My thoughts today are based on the lack of leadership/mentorship mentioned in the above book.

The priority of planning is a must in any business to continue with much-needed growth. I watched this as I silently listened to Edward, one of the members; his level of learning and his intentionality along the path of personality-building leaders turned his team members into stakeholders. Edward has built a great team of stakeholders yet is humble enough to accept advice.

Thoughts to Self:

a) Real Leaders are not threatened by people with great potential.

b) No executive has ever suffered because his people were strong and effective.

c) As a potential leader, you are either an asset or a liability to the organization.

d) Team leaders build the value of team members and team growth and, in turn, a great company.

e) It is vital to have a sense of humor to laugh and smile at your past. Then grow from the lesson and move to the next level of your journey.

'Black Spot'

"The black spot," a nice clear white piece of paper with a small black dot in the middle. We are drawn to pay attention and focus on the black dot. We focus on what is going wrong in our personal or business life. We are so fixated on the dot we forget the other 99 percent of the clear paper. The clear paper represents a reflection of everything else that is going right. As we remain transfixed on the dot, we remain focused on the small dot that looks bigger than it is. I am not suggesting to avoid the dot. I am advising not to give the dot more time than it deserves. Keep more focus on the white paper, the rest of the 99 percent.

'I have watched grown men go to their graves early due to too much focus on the black dot. Enjoy and live peacefully with the knowledge of only spending well-deserved time on what matters the most, family.'

'Most Important Day.'

The day I was born was the most important day of my life so I thought. On my birthday I was born on this earth to start my earthly life. When we are born we don't know that we are born. When I turned forty my thought process during many silent nights was what is my purpose here on earth. Why did God create me & what does God want me to do here on earth? During the months after turning forty one years old, I surrendered my Life to Jesus Christ. I was born again to live a second time; born again in spirit. Now, this was the most important day of my life & I was wide awake to feel the spirit enter my Heart.

At the start of forty one years old, and during the days that followed, I enjoyed "QT" time even more with myself a lot more.

'It's during these times that I got to understand that the loudest sound is the sound of silence when you get in touch with your inner self.'

What a moving joy as you connect with your soul and begin to understand why you are here on earth. My part is to make this world a better place every day by doing my best which can be as simple as speaking into a person's life. Then watching their face warm up as they finally get it. The warm joy of mentoring for positive transformation in one's life is such a feeling of the pure flame of love passing on.

'Reckless life.'

I have lived a crazy reckless life through my twenties and thirties, a life full of alcohol, full of self and pride. I lived blinded by darkness in the wilderness. I lived in the wilderness. I must say it was always about myself, my growth, and my arrogance, which was my fuel. When I broke my barrier of total silence, my still heart burst into true life. I felt the true joy of life, real life that was earth-shaking, and a simple whisper of God's love. This was when I gave my life to Jesus Christ as my personal saver in December 2011.

I was out of the wilderness, the desert. I felt alive in the wind, in the sun, in the rain, and on the grass within God's tender arms. I am now connected with my God with my purpose, which is still ongoing.

Along my path over the last twelve years, since I turned 40, I have lived a life of true growth. My life is balanced better, my growth is smoother, and my challenges are dealt with better understanding, and God is and has always been by my side.

'The real growth path was the transformation of the heart.'

BEFORE

I have lived many years through my thirties, and I have made lots of money in millions of dollars. I was able to build, and I built an empire, my company in Rwanda. Those were the days when I called myself self-made with total arrogance and full of pride as I took all the credit for my own abilities.

AFTER

Along my new God-given path, when I use the word 'I,' it only means it's associated with God this time. As I am one with God and God is in me, we have become ONE.

'Switched Gears'

I have switched gears with my new focus on the transformation of lives around me. I have supported the growing leaders around me, and the days of followers are gone. In the past, before my 40 years, my passion included having followers, but after 40 years, my passion has been building leaders. The leadership bug spreads to building other leaders. In turn, I strengthen myself with the leaders around me. I do not like prudent leaders who can only talk with zero action.

'True leaders lead to transform and benefit others as a part of their journey.'

"Leaders by action, powerful"

"Leaders by mouth, poor."

'It's only through hands-on experience that I am able to offer powerful mentorship, not just book experience.'

I mentor others to detect possible mistakes coming up. In this way, they can grow from the real valuable lessons I learned along this great journey.

'Over the days, the weeks, and the months, I look back and smile as my growth has only come from failure.'

Oh, and oh boy, I have failed in life so many times; it just makes me smile. I have been called names I cannot even write down on paper, been put in jail a few times, and had every material asset taken from me and stolen from me. I have carried the cross of a whole country's mistakes and bore the full force of this country Rwanda, hunting me down with life threats. But, my journey continues, and boy, have I grown during this great journey of failure turned into success.

I traveled a risky journey; I followed my passion, business, to bring change within myself and continued growth on all levels. As I read one of my many books today, I am learning about the one percent rule.

Basically, improve yourself by one percent every week. This is simple but powerful. As we have 52 weeks in a year, thus one can improve by 52% within one year, yes, one year.

I committed myself to follow the one percent rule with effect from July 1, 2016, meaning I committed to improving by 26% by the end of that year, December 2016. The weekly 1% improvement must have one's intentionality to improve. This is over and above one's daily activity. So, let's get going; see you at the end of December. I will be 26% better than I was today (keep in mind I am not at zero, but I will be 26% better as a person holistically by the end year).

'Find Silver go Looking….'

The song goes like this; If you want to find silver, go looking at the mountain…. If you want to find love….., go look at your home……., If you want to find heaven, go look in the Bible... *My add-in to the song…… 'If you want to find business, go looking for true entrepreneurs…..'* **'The risk takers, the job creators, and the visionaries to find your financial freedom.'**

'Vetting the People Giving advice.'

Friends, always ask yourselves from which experience and knowledge base you are getting your advice. Let me give you an example. If I face a personal issue and want advice from a specific person, I will ask myself: is this person married? Does this person have children? Or does this person believe in God? Based on the issue at hand, the advice will be short and unbalanced if the said person does not fulfill all of the above.

'Unbalanced advice can be and is very dangerous and can kill you.'

If you think cigarettes kill, try the unbalanced advice that you follow from a person who is coming from a place he/she has no knowledge of.

'Blind Pastors Leading the needy.'

During one of our Church services, our Pastor talked about finance with the topic of 'Prison Break.' The main focus was dealing with better planning and control of our financial future. I find the advice from our Pastor does not carry the credibility of valuable knowledge and insight.

'It's a huge shortcoming to pretend to know what you don't know.'

The Pastor was mostly talking to the congregation that is employed as he is also employed and would not have the depth to cover the same to those who employ the employees.

'We, the entrepreneurs, create wealth and employment. It's through the wealth of employment that we change nations for the better. It is also through employment that our Christian employees can pay Tithe to the church. '

I noticed his preaching was full of fear and full of the wrong advice on how to stay in mediocracy.

'No insight yet advice.'

As he preached, he talked about working until the retirement age of sixty-five years old, as it is in Kenya. As I look from a balanced knowledgeable point of view connected to the book we had been reading, 'Is Making Money Killing your Business.' One of the key lessons and goals within this powerful book was the value of training your staff members to become stakeholders. It's through specific steps within Three to Five Years that one's business will achieve its Business Maturity Date. We refer to this as our BMD. In this group made up of CEOs, we each give our BMD dates which must be between 3 to 5 years with a specific date and time. Yes, my company did achieve its BMD date and took my family on a one-week holiday on that day and time. *(My BMD date was 12/12/ 2015 at 12pm)* The main aim of the BMD is to have a company that runs automatically as the CEO takes a back seat.

'So, on the other hand, you have this Pastor coming to advise how to take life slowly on the advice of slow builds, pure laziness with no sense of using your own God-given talents.'

I strongly believe our men of the cloth should focus on their area of experience. When I want to better understand something I do not understand in the Bible, I seek advice from my Pastor Friends. In turn, business is an area a lot of men of the cloth have no experience in unless they have hands-on business experience.

'Let those who have a hands-on depth of experience lead those areas they are gifted in.'

An additional lesson learned from the same book is:

How to have 3 in 1. "Time, Money, and Energy."

Sorry Pastor, your way of advice on this one does not cut it at all.

'One of the best killers of our dreams is procrastination.'

The act of waiting and planning and then waiting and planning with no execution. I can assure you that you will fail, but just get up and grow from the experiences. When you grow from the experiences of failure, you have not failed but learned and grown. This is why 'Sometimes you Win, and sometimes you Learn.' When we learn the lesson, we grow.

'The only time you have failed is when you stop trying; then, you have really failed.'

I have been called several derogatory names during my huge failures over the past two decades. Pastors and former friends have distanced themselves and pulled away from me. Most importantly, my God pulled me closer to Him. I witness a lot of pastors play life safely to live average lives here on earth. Sadly I watch a lot of pastors defending the reason why they live poor lives as a form of honor.

'Friends, there is no honor in letting fear take the day when we should let faith with action's rule our days.'

When it comes to financing, ask yourself, does pastor "X" have the experience? The know-how? As one seeks advice, always keep an open thought process about what valuable experience this person has. If not, the advice is unbalanced; more value will come from a person through hands-on experience in the core area of interest. We only grow if we make mistakes.

'If we are not making mistakes, we are not growing. I will lessen with much deeper depth to one who has failed, failed, failed, and gotten up again and again.'

Our Savior Jesus was a risk-taker. He gave the ultimate prize, His life. Jesus is our true example of risk-taking, yet a lot of pastors feel they should live average lives and offer advice from a place of Fear, not Faith. One should always pay special attention to what area of experience the said person is coming from.

'One of our biggest dangers in life is getting advice from a person that does not have valuable hands-on experience about which they seek to provide advice.'

"Enjoy failure turned into Golden Growth!"

Thought builders to self:

- The team is not everything; the right team is everything.

- Let go of the team members that are no longer part of the vision statement.

- Then focus, drive forward, and do not waste time second-guessing yourself.

- My key role has been and must continue to be all about Vision, Vision, and Vision.

- Always push to stay above the noise, and enjoy growing and learning. I will no longer stay with the chickens but fly like the eagle I am and must be.

- Keep with your vision and never allow staff members to change your path, growth, and God-given gifts.

Successful Failures Lesson Take Away:

'Our belief in our mind is key to personal growth in this journey we call life. One must find their own path, as painful as this path may be. It is your path when you fail, and you will fail. **Stop, Pause, Learn and move on to the path ahead.** The Greater the challenge, the Greater the victory! Smile from the losses, challenges, the setbacks with those experiences you have grown'

Turn on a new leaf, and always grow from your Valuable Failures through experiences!

CHAPTER 4 – SILVER HAIR

Description: Scars into Stars.

"Silver Hair."

The silver hair on my head has increased as waves of life charges have washed over my soul. I always say there can be no change if we do not change. I see family and friends ask themselves why their lives remain the same year in and year out.

'It's simple; we must change to get the change we want to get.'

This is a daily journey with small baby steps every day. At the end of the month, this yields big steps and at the end of each year yields a huge giant step of positive change.

'It's through this change that I always say, 'If it is meant to be, it's up to me.' We must seek the change we would like to be.'

It is simple; a change in attitude is all that is needed. A change in attitude will lead to a change in our habits. Let's keep in mind our small daily habits give us direction in our life.

'One must refocus one's lenses. In the same way, once we adjust our focus on our camera, we see different objects differently.'

What we see, we attract back to ourselves. When we adjust and look at life differently we will seek the different positive results we yearn for.

It's from my failed marriage, that I was Blessed with two beautiful kids, now young adults as I finish writing my book. The upturn from my failed business resulted in even greater business, this time around, with God in it.

'Through the years, my silver hair has turned my sight to see the silver lining in my new marriage and my new business.'

As the silver grows, I grow with joy and better understanding into a greater person on the personal and business sides.

'The happiness of joy, true joy comes from true peace'.

Where do we find peace?

We find peace right within ourselves. The Bible tells us, "Seek, and you will find." The challenge we face, I face, is we do not slow down to seek. When we slow down to close our eyes and slow down our breathing, we can feel and see peace. We can all attain joy and balanced healing through peace.

'The growth of peace comes from forgiveness. First of ourselves, then others.'

As we forgive, we grow and feel the weight lifted off our shoulders. The word forgiveness is the way of releasing and letting go to allow more space for love. This means we intentionally block out love because we do not want to forgive. We tend to sometimes think that not forgiving someone is a sign of one's strength, but it's the other way around. The act of forgiving is the true strength embedded into our souls.

'The solutions to our challenges are within us, within our subconscious mind. Tap into this great God-given power to draw out your greatness.'

We have the power to break bad habits and the same power to grow good habits. Friends, we are created in the image of our God. This means we have the power within. We actually do not want to use our

God-given powers. I have seen how many family members and friends focus on letting fear hold them back. In most cases, they let fear rule the day instead of acting on their faith.

"Overriding thought "

In life, we will have enemies for many different reasons. Let's keep in mind enemies are mostly from family and friends in the past as your life takes a different path, as it always will after schooling, as you start your journey of building your own life. Some family members and friends will become envoys of you as you push forward. It's simple to tell who is for you and who is against you.

These are the two different groups:

> 1). Group ONE: When Good News Spreads of something positive you have done.

> The different Group members for you will call you with excitement to congratulate you.

> 2). Group TWO: When Bad News Spreads of something negative that has happened to you.

> The different group members will call you like they are concerned. Friends, they are not concerned; they want to hear of your pain; it makes them feel better.

> If they did not call or communicate during your Good News, then know they are not calling out of concern. They will pretend they are but trust me; they are not.

We must learn the silent power in dealing with one's enemies. Our enemies will try everything possible to bring us down, to try to destroy us and to get us below their level.

'This brings them joy because it makes them feel better and look better, so they think.'

Our enemies are filled with negative energy and very quick at spreading the negative energy through rumors. This is what feeds them; they enjoy it, and it drives them.

'Friends, focus on your life and the positive daily steps forward. Be like a racehorse with blinders on the sides of its eyes with a forward focus only.' As you keep the focus on your active victory and turn your back on them, these actions will destroy your enemies.

'Once you have overcome your current enemies, they will switch focus to look for someone else. Imagine this is exactly how the devil works.'

Once the devil sees you no longer believe in his lies, he gives up on you and goes looking for someone else. As you bounce back into Victory over Victory, 'Group Two' will never like to discuss your comeback. Avoid these people at all costs as they are heading nowhere and would like you to join them on the nowhere journey.

During one of my moments with my Queen, my best friend, my honey, and my wife, Jennifer told me she admired how I handled my enemies & Frenemies. She admires me for how I have been able to protect my inner Peace from my enemies and frenemies.

'Our inner Peace is what our foes come for.'

As a warrior, I fight for Peace daily, and I always keep my mental detector switched on.

One very important additional quality one needs in life is to take time to listen to what the other person is saying. The solution is always in the problem itself.

'Once you become a true listener, you will become a true problem solver.'

I have also been able to wisely overcome many of my enemies over the years through my keen listening. While one's listening, you will pick out the problem and turn this problem into the solution at hand.

'It's vital to stay cool and focused in order to have your victory by picking out the solution.'

Let the other side feel like the solution came from them if need be. At the end of the day, for the task at hand, either way, you will have won.

'A New Leaf'

Today is a brand-new day, a brand-new month, and a brand-new year 2018. What a wonderful feeling it is. God, I look back at the last year and smile as I sit here in my beautiful garden, enjoying my cup of tea.

'We tend to forget the great victories within a very short time.'

Today is my day to pause and reflect on the victory achieved in 2017. The most part of 2017 was filled with incoming shareholders playing dirty, evil games to try and reap where they have not sowed. These had been shareholders who did not even pay for their shares in full. When I look back at my past year, 2017, I am able to better understand that one needs to vet the possible incoming shareholders beforehand.

'It's imperative to know that the solution sometimes is not just about the money.'

When we tend to narrow our focus, we only get narrow options on the table. This limits our growth due to limiting our options.

'We close the doors in our lives and then ask God why, what is it that I have done wrong?'

Friends, this has nothing to do with God but more so the fact that a lot of times, we miss God's message. I know the next question is, how come I do not hear God's message?

'It's simple because we do not spend quiet time with God alone.'

Trust me; God has the time anytime. The issue at hand is our own selves. In life and in business, we always have numerous solutions. Once we take time to have time to pause and think and plan, the solutions will be right in front of us.

"We must all know that sometimes we Win, and Sometimes we Learn."

We never lose if we learn the lesson. Yes, each and every experience, positive or negative, has a lesson. Over the years, based on the painful experience, I have learned to pause and ask myself what the lesson is here.

'The sign of growth and leadership comes when we learn from the experience.'

You become mature when you learn the art of patience. In patience and the quiet time comes the insight of our God-given powers. Our God has equipped us with all that we need, and we just have to tap into our powers within.

'As in the Good Book, *"Ask, and you will receive, knock, and the door will be opened."*

Guess what? We become afraid to knock; then we ask God why the door is locked!

'Fear comes from within, from family, and from close friends.'

This same Fear that is brought on or reflected on should propel us forward and not hold us back. I ask myself, when faced with a specific challenge do I feel the fear? If yes, this is great, for I want to face my fears and grow from them. I feel the fear and do it anyway.

'As you face your Giants head on, one's Fears will step aside to allow Faith take on the fight with you.'

'The key point is Fear does not come from God but from the devil.'

The devil uses all possible tricks through family, friends, and within ourselves.

'The devil enjoys it as he watches fear hold us back and not use our God-given gifts. Our God has given us glory, favor, love, and grace, yet we choose Fear.'

In the Bible, the word 'Fear not' is used 365 times, and we have 365 days. Do you think it's coincidental? This means each day uses faith to bring down fear. If God is for you, really, who can be against you? Do not let the devil take the day.

So today, on January 1, 2018, I use the first 'Fear not. I will keep pushing forward to get my book published and get my messages out. This book, 'My Successful Failures,' even as I am told by family members and so called friends, not to do so.

'Keep in mind their advice is coming from a place of fear.'

The fear that holds them back they try to pass onto me to hold myself back. I will not let the devil win.

'I push forward day by day to show God's power in me.'

The steps of achievement, the steps of joy, the steps of tears, the steps of failures, and the steps of success have turned into steps of growth.

'My continued journey is a mixed blend of joyful, painful, and successful grace of growth.'

I ponder many times a month as I gaze out at the painful experiences of my growth as evil forces tried to stop me.

'The tears that stream down my face have built me into a stronger, well-balanced man.'

"Successful Failures Key Lesson"

About 25 years ago, I went skiing in Vermont, USA. I was so eager to get on top of the different slopes and start skiing. This was my first-time trying out skiing. I went with my American cousins, who had many years of experience.

There, before me, was white snow set on the high mountains, great slopes, and my young blood pumping on bring it on. After all, I was only 25 years old. After breakfast, I was super ready as we all dashed to the ski resort check-in point. At this point, I was saddened when I was told by one of the ski instructors, "if you have not skied before, you must start with the bunny slopes."

My cousins went in one direction, and I took the direction toward the short small bunny slopes. This affected me as I was angry; why would I ski with young kids? Why? This is just wrong! Then we got started, and with each try, I was down on my rear end. Some of the little kids made it look easy, yet for me, this was just too difficult and super embarrassing.

The ski instructor walked up to me and told me the first lesson was to learn how to fall down. Over the next hour, I was taught and learned how to fall and enjoy falling. Having learned this powerful lesson, the rest of the day was a day filled with fun. I was able to start skiing on the different levels of bunny slopes. This was a great day because I learned in life, we must learn how to fall.

'Once we learn how to fail and pick ourselves up each time, we keep growing.' Those young kids had learned the value of having fun in falling and, in turn, improved their skills.

The key life lesson is that falling/failing will happen but learn how to best do so. When it happens, and it will happen, you have just turned your failure into success. This is because failing is succeeding, as you learn the lesson.

Over 25 years later, this lesson has remained one of the core building blocks in my mind. This lesson has formed into a part of me, both on the business side and personal side. Over the years, I have taught my kids how to ride their bicycles and any other outdoor activities. The first lesson I teach them is how to fall. Once they learn how to fall over a few lessons, they pick up the activity with ease and great joy; when they do fall, they are better prepared with a key lesson on how to best fall.

'Dad's Mistakes'

Over the last years of my dad's life, I watched him beat himself up mentally due to his past mistakes. This took my dad to this grave before his time. As I have seen so many people filled with anger over past mistakes over the years. Instead of focusing their energy on the lesson learned, they focus on regret. The regret builds up into bitterness. My dad's anger and bitterness destroyed him from the inside.

'I look at all my failures as successful failures based on lessons learned. I can't change the past, but I can change the future, which is even more important.'

The value that one needs to know is we each have the power to change our tomorrow through learning the lessons of our yesterday.

Over the years, my forties have given me a panoramic bird's eye view of my personal and business life.

'My maturity of Wisdom has come of age where I am able to look at myself and laugh, and this is very healthy.'

My past successful failures stretch back into the last three decades. My lessons learned have sweetened my passion for mentoring young men and women. This has given birth to my mentorship company called "Seed of Success." The key difference is mentorship from hands-on experience.

'The hurts and the cries build us into who we are if we grow from them!'

'Wife to Ex-Wife to Foe'

As I sit here at home in my cool garden, I think, I smile, and I imagine the turmoil I have gone through. It's been seven years of hardship, seven years in the wilderness.

'Friends, it's been hard; my heart was broken into a thousand pieces as my ex-wife now Cleophase turned from friend to foe.'

As my ex-Rwandese wife joined the critics with insults over me, as she distanced herself from me like I was the plague, my spirit was tested to the core, but I have come out on top only by God's Grace and Mercy over me.

'My broken heart has been pieced back together, and my soul and spirit have strengthened. I am a better, smarter, and wiser man with peace at the center.'

I have gained spiritual experience and mental growth. Having moved on from the heartbreaking experiences, I still need to improve daily.

'I have always taken the road less traveled in my life. It has been bumpy, it has been rough, it has been heartbreaking, but most importantly, looking

back, it has been worth it.'

This is because this has drawn me closer to who I have now become. I am, and I continue to depend on, my God-given talents to make this world around me a better place.

"Do not neglect your God-given gifts that are in you. My experiences from failure have turned me into Solid Gold.

'I have used the rocks that were thrown at me to build my house, my home, and my family.'

What the devil planned through the devil's people has turned what was meant for harm into my Gold Victories.

'Turning Scars Into Stars'

I had to go through the fire, through the testing, through the growth to come out on top. I am better, smarter, wiser, simpler, and humbler and turned into a solid gold personality. I have a better heart, a better understanding, and a better wife, and I am just a better human being. Added to this, my new wife, Mrs Jennifer Loyd is a deep God-Fearing wife. We are also Blessed with our beautiful daughter Jasmine Lindy Loyd who is currently a six-years-old daughter.

"Distorted Fear."

We cover it up, call it by different names, dance around it and avoid using the word Fear. We like to say words like it was not safe; We say we could have done it a different way. At the end of the day, it all boils down to Fear, Period.

'Only a few ordinary men can face Fear with faith. Without a doubt, brave men and women are entrepreneurs; these are a special breed. I am one of those breeds to Feel Fear and do it anyway.'

I do feel fear as I have traveled for the past thirty years, the road less traveled. Friends, even the so-called men of cloth, show the deepest Fear, yet they should be showing the Greatest Faith. On the business side, do remember to seek advice from those who are in business and with a preference ahead of you. It would be very misplaced to seek business advice from a Pastor that has no depth into what this involves. In most cases, the business advice given will be coming from a place of Fear, and this will not benefit you in any way.

'We, the trailblazers, the job providers, are the true Heroes that are overlooked yet criticized the most.'

In the Bible, 'Fear not' is used 365 times, and we have 365 days. This is a clear reference that tells us to use one ' Fear not' each day and replace it with 'faith' daily.

'Talk with Action'

As I look back on my past business years, I smile, for I have never feared failing. I may not have taken the needed time to plan ahead. In my younger years, mainly in my thirties, I used to jump in without planning. However, I learned the lesson and value of planning and going into action. The focus is on the action, not just simple talk or planning and planning with no action. I have grown into a better version of myself deeper into my forties. I plan more and act more and then chase down my dreams daily. One of my favorite sayings is, *'Sometimes You Win, and Sometimes You Learn.' We never lose if we learn the lesson. Now that is Great News to know.*

Friends, do not let Fear hold you back, have active faith and step in. This will give you your freedom. God has given each of us our own Talents. Learn quickly to find out what your talent is and use it to make your life better and those around you.

The light will always chase away the darkness.

'On the same note, faith will always chase away Fear.'

Always keep a keen eye, watch out for who is offering advice and keep your mind alert if the advice is coming from Fear. Friends, even Pastors, can have Fear overtake their faith. In this case, do not allow their words of Fear to overcome you. We have each been created in the image of our God. Since our God is a Powerful God and we are in His image, it means we are powerful. Go for it and overcome the Fear you will feel the joy of the sweet Victory on the other side.

'A lot of times, we are taught by those closest to us to let our fears rule our days.'

This can come from the fact that those trying to advise us to operate from a level of fear. Since they have not been able to overcome their own fears, they want you to join them. It's these same people who sit on the sidelines that are quick to point out the faults and mistakes of the Go-Getters. Keep in mind that nothing is impossible; we are only limited by ourselves.

"For God has not given us a spirit of fear, but of power and love and of a sound mind" (2 Timothy 1:7)

Friends enjoy the fearless falling towards the experience of true growth through faith. "When you see it, you can seek it."

"Turned The Page."

I turned the page yesterday from age forty-seven to forty-eight. I bid farewell to 47 and welcomed 48.

What have I enjoyed from my last year? I paused, I thought, I looked and smiled; I am in atonement with God. I am 'at-one-ment' with God.

> My God gives me strength.

> My God gives me wisdom.

> My God gives me understanding.

> My God gives me peace.

> My God gives me love.

'Peaceful Proud'

As I unpause my blended emotions, I look at my beautiful wife, Jennifer, and into my kids' eyes and feel an explosion of peace. I am peacefully proud of who I have become and continue to become.

"Staying Power."

Friends, staying power is a must to learn from one's successful failures. When you fail, you will pick yourself up and try again. This time around, you become smarter and wiser once you have learned the lesson.

'Travel light, travel free, fill the punch and learn the lesson.'

Those who might claim they are not failing means that they are not trying at all. I see nothing great for those who proudly say they played life safe. I see no honor, for it amounts to a flat life.

During the decade of my twenties and thirties, between the years 1990 to 2010, I was busy pushing for every possible business opportunity. I traveled the Globe pushing from one business deal to another business deal. In my ventures over the two decades, I failed numerous times. I become better at failing by quickly learning the lesson. To the naked eye on the outside one looks in to point out how I failed at so many business ventures. To my clear eagle's eye, I smile at the growth of the journey of my successful failures. It's through these failures that I have been a trailblazer of success in thousands of people's lives.

"It is important and vital to travel light, focus on the future and let go of the past."

"Fear of Failure."

"Success is Never ending; Failure is Never Final" – Dr. Robert Schuller.

Great quotes:

- *Most people fail because they haven't tried.*

- *Those who try have already succeeded in a very important area of life, for they have conquered the Fear of failure.*

- *I'd rather attempt to do something great and fail than attempt to do nothing and succeed.*

Wait a minute!

I really can't recall if I have ever been fearful when it came to business. I have been called a risk-taker and a Go-getter. Yes, I have failed several times. As I grew deeper into my forties and through my forties, I grew in wisdom from my valuable successes but more so from my failures. I smile with peace and joy, for the hardships have built me into a resilient person. My smile comes from deep in my heart, from the bedrock of the challenges that have molded me into the man I am. My painful successful failures have molded me into an extraordinary man.

The past seven years, by 2018, had molded me into a new man, a new person, and a new spirit. I was also Blessed with my new love in the form of my new wife Jennifer Loyd in 2016. My Love, My Honey, My Queen, My Lady, none other than Mrs. LOYD. My new appreciation of my total and fully depending on God and God alone grew and grew.

My heart, my fears, and my worries have all been covered with love, forgiveness, and peaceful joy!

'The deep scars, the scratches in my heart, in my smile, and in my soul have been turned into stars of gold.'

I am a better, reshaped, rebuilt, born-again gifted child of God. My scars are my stars. My internal scars have molded me into who I am as I continue on my journey here on earth. It is only from my painful lessons learned that I am able to offer valuable advice and mentorship, which I do.

Thought to Self:

"God already placed in us all that we need to use to succeed. We need to use our God-given gifts and stop finding excuses, including blaming God."

Our God has done His part, it's on you, and I to do our part.

"It is simple, change your thought process, and your life will change."

"If you think you can or think you can't, either way, you are right. We really do have the power within us."

Believe, and your belief will create the fact. (William James)

Successful Failures Lesson Take Away:

'As the silver increased in my head with more silver hair, my wisdom grew. I have learned the value of peaceful understanding. I have learned the value of growth from failure. I have learned the value of accomplishing growth through painful experiences. I had learned that even when my business failed and my marriage failed, my success continued. This stems from the fact I took time to learn the lesson and grow into a better, wiser, and more balanced man'.

Chapter 5 - Quiet Time

Description: Victory Hour

The value of 'Quiet Time' or 'QT.'

Note to self. QT or Quiet Time is essential for you to get in touch with your soul. It's essential to have quiet time as much as possible. I always make sure to plan my week with the most important at hand before daybreak, Quiet Time. As a matter of fact, out of a seven-day week, I must have a minimum of five days a week with QT time.

'During this precious moment, this Golden hour, you can't have any phone or gadget with you.'

This is where you can hear yourself breathing. All slows down, and you feel the stillness in the air. On my part, my phones and gadgets are clear across in another room. We must grow ourselves daily to get in touch with our core to fully better understand who we are. The importance of Quiet time with no phones or with no gadgets, no distractions, just enjoying the simplicity of being with yourself. During this time, I spend a smooth 20 minutes reading my Bible and another 20 minutes in total silence, and 20 minutes in thought and planning. As I write this page, I'm sitting in my tree house at home in Kenya with the gentle breeze kissing my cheeks. It's my daughter's tree house. I always look and find different spots. In this case, in my daughter's treehouse, I remain hidden and alone with myself. I gaze at the leaves dancing in the breeze and look at my garden below. My lush green garden with different colored flowers is just romantic. In the corner of my garden are my different animals, like rabbits, pigeons, and guinea pigs.

'Animals Jumping Around'

I remain gazed at my animals as they jump around with so much joy. The joy of just jumping around and around. A large warm smile comes across my cheeks as I see their joy. I marvel at how animals have learned the art of enjoying simple moments every single day. On the other hand, we humans start a life full of joy and adventure like little bunnies for the first few years of our lives. Then step by step, we complicate our lives even as early as adolescence. As adolescence, we start getting so distracted by gadgets. We start to pull away from the simple moments more and more. We then become accustomed to complaining about our lives and don't even enjoy spending time with ourselves.

'What is perplexing is how much fun simplicity is. We stop jumping around as human begins'.

The simple joy of jumping around has become so rare that when we see someone doing so we tend to think or ask what's wrong with that person.

Added to how great this is for our own health. It's a known fact that the number of ailments that come from stress and this takes a huge toll on our health. We face issues like high blood pressure that are caused by our lifestyle. I hear people use words like, 'that's just life.' How crazy is this that we have become blinded that sometimes I hear people say words like "it's life." The reference is that it is just the way life's meant for me, complicated and full of stress. On the other hand, I am sure animals do not have to deal with high blood pressure or other ailments from stress. Does this mean we, as the human race, know what we need to do but ignore the warning signs? Yet, animals do not know what to do yet have found one of the secrets in life, keeping it simple.

How do you start your Day?

When we wake up, the first task we rush to get our phones and our gadgets; some even switch on the news to try and get the latest updates. We fill our fresh, powerful minds with news that is usually filled with what is made to look like an emergency and like the world is coming to an end. We let in so much sad news at the start of our day, causing us to be unproductive daily. I watch with sadness how people I know fill their days with fear of nonsense from the time they wake up and grab their phones. Having their phones in hand they bend forward like zombies for hours on end looking over for the most part rubbish. I see hundreds of necks bent over for hours on end to find and listen to the latest updates on their phones. The sad part is 99% of the time; this only builds up our anxiety. This is what you feed your mind.

'Keeping in mind in life, whatever you focus on grows within us daily.'

My policy is to monitor and control what I do in the first waking hours of my day, which is from 5:30 am Monday to Friday. I did face a setback connected with my health during the years 2021 and 2022. This was mainly related to my sleep apnea, which has affected my timetable. Nonetheless, as I bounce back, I still make sure to have my victory hour; even if I wake up late, be it 6:30 am or 7 am. I will have my me-time with prayer time, where I will block off everything else and all distractions for one hour. I also faced a major, major surgery with removing a huge carotid tumor on the left side of my neck in December 2021. These events sometimes put my Victory hour on hold or pushed it forward by about an hour.

Our positive growth of getting to know oneself cannot be taken away by anyone, unless you allow it.

'Victory Golden Hour'.

The Peaceful Victory Hour is the time to fall in love with yourself, laugh about yourself, and grow as a person. This time is short, sweet, and powerful during the power hour. Connecting with my soul daily has given me a strength from within that builds me up every day. The victory hour is filled with the power of connecting with ourselves, with our God. This can only take place when there is no one around, and there are no electronics at all. I make it difficult to want to switch on my phones or gadgets by placing them away from me. In my case, it will take me two minutes to walk over and switch on my phones for the day. I tell you that it may be hard at first to train yourself in this positive habit.

'However, it is a wonderful feeling to spend time with your maker and yourself.'

It's only during this time that true leaders build and strengthen themselves.

In one of the books I read by Robin Sharma, "The 5 am Club," in this book, one learns the value of kick-starting our day at 5 am, that one hour of victory. In this daily one-hour victory, we have 20 minutes of activity to get your heart racing and do some cardiovascular exercise. Next, 20 minutes of Prayer and Reflection. That is the time to reflect and write in your journal if need be as you spend time on your planning and self-reflection. Then the last 20 minutes are the time of growth, and to know how to grow from this? This is through asking yourself questions. Like, how do I learn from this? What did I learn yesterday? No mistake is bad at all; in fact, it is great to learn the valuable lesson present within the so-called mistake.

'Sometimes We Win, and Sometimes We Learn. It's that simple.'

This is the very reason I am writing this book. "My Successful Failures." We must grow from failures alone by seeking to understand the lesson. It is through failure that we learn and grow. How joyful one should feel once one learns the lesson. *'Unfortunately, some people don't learn and grow, for they refuse to learn the lesson. These people switch to blaming others for their failure or the world at large. This does no good but holds one back from daily growth.'*

The sad part is, instead of moving forward for the better, they move into bitterness. They move into becoming very bitter and regretting the mistakes they made. They would not be mistakes if we learned the lessons. Sometimes we learn, and sometimes we grow if we learn the lesson. Once we learn the lesson, we're able to grow and then expand our minds and our vision.

It's Interesting that 90% of the world's population does not value this special POWER GOLDEN one hour. However, the 10% that value this one early hour, THE Victory Hour, the Golden Hour, THE hour that you connect with your Soul, THE hour that you Grow, THE hour that you build yourself, Are the 10% rule and control the world. The 10% that kick start their early morning, as the other 90% enjoy an extra hour of sleep, control the other 90%. This 10% live better and enjoy their lives better by controlling the first hour of their days.

'This builds into a habit, and once a good habit is hard-wired in your brain, you enjoy life a whole lot better.'

Starting your day right will automatically lead to a much more effective and manageable day.

'Set your victory hour as your first task every morning before the day breaks and before the sun is up. This is the time and only time when you will feel the peace of being alive within the very simplicities of life.'

Do not dare switch on any gadget at all during this Victory hour. Give it a try. I have a policy of switching my phones off. On weekdays I am off air on my phones from 7 pm to 7 am to mark 12 hours Monday to Friday. Then, come Saturday; I switch off by 5 pm to remain offline for 24 hours until 5 pm on Sunday.

'Once I am disconnected from this world of destruction, I connect to my world of wealth from within, my family, and my soul.'

Watching the news daily adds no value to my growth. It adds no value to what I would do to change the news but only builds anxiety. I can instead focus on changing myself and on building myself to become a better and better me. It's interesting that during my search and my quiet time, I got to find the most special person in the world. Yes, Myself. Get to enjoy spending time with yourself to enjoy yourself and grow from within.

Interesting question to ponder; Who are the Top Ten people you would like to meet in your lifetime?

We go down the list, including myself, in the past and never talk about meeting ourselves. What joy I found over the years in meeting myself daily during my quiet time. It's pure joy to have fun getting to know yourself.

My favorite number is three, and the third person I met and continue to enjoy spending time with is myself. Ladies and gentlemen, when you get to spend time with yourself, do not criticize yourself but love yourself. It is a wonderful feeling. We seem to enjoy being so difficult and hard on ourselves. Remember, we are only human and here on earth to make this world a better place as we enjoy our time here on earth.

'It's sad as we sometimes tend to think that meeting oneself or loving oneself, or taking care of oneself is looked at negatively.'

I've met some fellow Christian brothers, especially those who think that the component of loving yourself is very wrong. Boy, I can tell you they are wrong with distorted thinking of life. I have been asked several times, "how can you say that you like to take time off to go for a pedicure or manicure and massage?" I tell them, "Yes, I actually dedicate a whole day, twice a month, for me-time beautification time and taking care of myself. The act of taking care of myself builds me up into a better, more enjoyable person to be around. I look forward to these times twice a month and set these times on my calendar as appointments. After all, if you do not take care of yourself, who else will do so?

"It's your life; take time for yourself."

Otherwise, you will burn out. When you avoid taking care of yourself, the next task you will be doing is spending time at the doctor's office paying the doctor's bills. One ends up dealing with other issues, including high blood pressure and other complications from the simple failure of avoiding ourselves.

"Our state of mind and how we treat ourselves physically, mentally, and spiritually are directly connected to our current health, positively or negatively."

Imagine having five victory hours every week? Yes, every week, and then multiply this by 50 weeks of the year. This equals a powerful 250 direct hours per year of growth and betterment of yourself. Even with a Monday-to-Friday focus, one power hour per day gives you five hours per week to put you in better shape on all levels. Having a better connection can lead and direct you in a better direction before the world has woken up and before any distractions. I switch off my phones at 7 pm to disconnect from distractions and, in turn, to enjoy time with those who matter the most to me, my direct family. I have made this into a habit with my phone disciple at least 90% of the time between Monday to Friday every week. I will not switch my phones back on until 7 am or 7:30. In this way, through this disciple, I have beat the distractions that do not build me up in any way.

"It's only during my Victory/Golden One Hour Per Day; My Direction is set for the rest of my day."

Usually, between 7:30 am and 8 am, I also enjoy, for the most part, taking my kids to school as this forms a special bonding time with them. On these days, I will switch my phone on at around 8 am to avoid distractions during my time with my kids on the way to school. Or I place my phone on Airplane mode for thirty minutes. My Kids need Daddy's attention, and I need to listen to them to respond in a best-balanced way. Once done with a warm smile, I switch on to connect to the world.

'CEO Biggest Challenge'

At this point, I pick up my current role as CEO of my company 'AvoVeg health.'

One of my biggest challenges is getting my staff members to be in tune with my company's Vision and Mission Statement and our Core Values. This is connected to the ownership of each staff member's roles and duties. My focus continues on how I can mentor my staff members into being better leaders than myself. In turn, building better leaders than myself is the true test of leadership skills. As a leader, I also draw the line to make sure I do not do their job duties. Once hired, performance must check in for their specific purpose to handle their specific roles and duties. The normal tendency for a lot of staff is to be lazy, and laziness checks in as they try to hide behind you as the owner and make the owner do the work.

'Key Golden Hour Pillar'

One of the key pillars that are vital is understanding the value of the golden hour. During our golden hour, every aspect is covered with 20 minutes of activity, 20 minutes of reflection/Prayer, general internal reflection, and 20 minutes of planning for growth. The golden hour totals up to 60 minutes. I added another 30 minutes for power emails. Having a start time of 5:30 am will mean that by 7 am, I am done with the most important part of my day. Then I am ready to face the rest of my day with all controls in place.

'It's a wonderful feeling to start and kick-start your day before your day really starts.'

In addition, I plan twice a week to focus for 3 hours on emails. I keep a keen eye on delegating to my staff members to handle their roles and duties. It's imperative not to start responding to emails sent out to my staff members as this will turn the table from the employer becoming the employee. In addition pulls away ownership of the staff member's to take on their roles and duties.

Successful Failures Lesson Take Away:

"Remember, you get out what you put in daily. As you go along your day, switch on your mental detector; when negative thoughts come, delete them, and when positive thoughts come, build on them."

My Successful Failures

CHAPTER 6 - AMBITION

<u>Description: Go for it</u>

"Ambition the Power of the Few."

Ladies and gentlemen, there is nothing wrong when failures come from ambition. The key here in ambition means that one is making an effort. One is taking the steps forward to make a difference in their area of interest. It means that you have tried different tasks with assorted risks along the way. You have tried to make a difference in your different fields and aspects.

"It's those that are ambitious in life, the go-getters, that get criticized the most by those who do the list & a lot of times do nothing but point fingers".

Keep this in mind if you are getting criticized a lot; this is a good sign you are going after your dreams. On the other hand, the non-doers will be your biggest critics. These can be, and a lot of times, are even family members and so-called friends that have given up on their dreams. The best thing this group tries to do is have you join them by giving up on your own dreams. It's easy to spot this group. They are finger pointers, always quick to advise how they would have handled a specific situation differently from you. So you have the ones who play life safe, able to try and offer advice from a non-doer. Note the key component is how they would have done it differently. Keep in mind they did not even try but have become the experts in nonsense.

'This group of so-called experts, always ready to point out one's mistakes, add no positive value to your life. They have achieved nothing in whatever career path they have, yet are quick to point out your failures'.

I personally have been an entrepreneur and businessman for the past thirty years as I pushed to finish my book in 2022. I have been involved in the minerals business in Congo for several years, the construction business in Rwanda for several years, and the Agricultural business in Kenya for several years. I have had the pleasure of making a huge difference in thousands of lives across Congo, Rwanda, and Kenya. These thousands of individuals have gone on to benefit their whole households with a continuous positive impact. The 99% Good I have done on this earth is not mentioned. But Boy, you can see how the 1% negative is blown up to make it look like I was all about the 99% negative. I urge you to take heart because the critics are the non-doers trying to make themselves feel better.

"Do take note, nowhere in the World will you find a Monument of a Critic"

These are our true heroes. In my view, about 90% of the world that we live in plays it safe. Playing it safe has become a component where we hold ourselves back out of fear. One decides that one would rather not try and venture into the unknown. It is in this venture of the unknown that we find our God-given Gifts. The sad part is that in your gut, you want to try and go for it, but you allow fear to hold you back. The fear holds one back the first Day in, which turns into Week in, then deeper into Month in, and further into Year In. As fear steps in, we lose focus on what someone will say if we fail at it.

'My words of advice, confirm and Feel the Fear and Go for it.'

Yes, tell yourself I feel the Fear. Yes, face the fact of how Fear makes you feel. You want to try this venture and want to give it a go. You want to experience this thrill; however, your focus shifts more to what if you fail and what people will think if you fail. What if this happens or that happens, and the list goes on and on…

'One of the key secrets to success is to double your failures.'

Failure is part of life. If you are not failing and growing from the lessons learned, that means you are doing nothing but pointing figures. Yes, you can gain wisdom from others who have gone before you and do it their way with a twist of what you can do differently to further enhance the outcome. The fact that our population is increasing means our needs and wants will keep increasing. This fact alone means your opportunities are waiting to be called out. One's role here is to face your Fears and search for your own opportunity.

'Face the fact you will fail; just learn to bounce back through your daily growth from Failure. Once the lesson is learned from one's 'successful failures,' it is a clear sign that you are growing.'

Enjoy the journey of life through growing from lessons learned. It's through the lessons learned that we become better at what we do.

We have to find different ways to grow, different ways to improve, and different ways to face different challenges in life.

'In ambition, go after your dreams actively every single day. Find your passion and push forward.'

Remember, "Feel the Fear, and Do IT anyway." Move away from just talking about your plans alone and be a Doer.

'There is nothing wrong with fear but never allow fear to hold you back, never.'

Learn the lesson and grow from the fear. If you do not feel the fear, you are playing safe and sitting on the sidelines.

"Door Mats."

I have seen, and I have been, a doormat for many years to many people. We tend to misread the meaning behind the word in the Bible: humility. I have, and we tend to think the act of being humble is good, for this connects with the value of our humility. Over the years this has become clear to me that humility does not mean you allow everyone to walk all over you. In humility, one needs a true blend of confidence. Humility does not mean one should say yes and agree to everything. I have walked down this path of always trying to please everyone for the sake of humility. Yes, over the years, numerous family members, friends, and enemies have taken advantage of my humility. Friends, I have now learned that one needs to have humility with confidence.

'Great Pride is Positive'

As Christians, a lot of us have turned to think that confidence is prideful. I am here to tell you now that it is pure rubbish.

'We are created in His image with the power vested in our chests. Let's act like and be like the Warriors God created us to be.'

We do so and act like our Savior, Jesus Christ, Bold, Humble, and Confident. We remain respectful, humble, and confident, knowing all Victory and Glory goes to God.

Do not allow, as I did in the past, to be used as a doormat. The word itself means allowing people to rub off all their dirt and issues on you to solve. Keep in mind you have your own personal issues to solve. These groups of friends and family just want to throw all their rubbish to you to solve as they make no changes in their own personal lives.

There is nothing wrong with saying a simple No, or I really do not agree with you, or I really see it differently; this lets you take back your identity. Once you are able to handle what you can handle, let the other party handle their part. The firmness out of Love with confident humility will put a stop to getting used as a doormat.

"My Valuable Experiences in Life"

Today is another wonderful day. I'm sitting again in one of my wonderful hiding spots, my daughter's treehouse. I enjoy this spot because, in the smoothness of nature, my thoughts start to flow. My current thought is on the thought of valuable learned experience. Once we face our mountains with total confidence to learn from the mountain before you. Then you have overcome your fear of this mountain and are ready to face the next and the next.

"Epidemic Heroes"

As I sit here at home in my garden, during this very difficult time due to Covid19, for Kenya and the world at large, a beaming thought comes to mind that no weapons can fight this virus, and even churches around the world come to a stop.

Who are the real heroes?

Who are the true risk-takers?

Who is putting food on the table for hundreds, thousands, and even millions of people here in Kenya and around the world?

'Friends, the true bonafide tested heroes are the entrepreneurs.'

I am not talking about the business people that have only taken advantage of this epidemic for self-gain. The self-gain is a temporary measure when one only looks out for self. I am talking about the ones that stay the course for the sake of their business, and in turn, this puts food on the table for families around the world. We find solutions to better our lives for the betterment of millions around the world. I am talking about the ones who stay up late at night and get up early in the morning to make sure their team members have a job. It's through this job each person is able to provide food on the table. These

"We are the true unsung Heroes of our world at large, the Leaders in real transformation and economic change. I am proud to be one of the true Heroes."

This epidemic we face, Covid-19, has only strengthened my relationship with God. God has shown me the power within the gifts of facing our mountains. I am even more alert when I face fear or worry.

"I look Fear in the eye boldly, and I say get out of here!!!!. I am a child of God, created in His image. Fear not, for I am with you, says the Lord."

I am, and I have the True Spirit of the Warrior that I have become a True Leader, a True Father, & a true provider.

Successful Failures Lesson Take Away:

'The Heroes of our world are the doers, the risk-takers, and the go-getters. The entrepreneurs who brave the cold nights, who brave the threats, and who never take no for an answer. I am One of the Few'

Chapter 7 - True Friends

Description: Tainted Vision

I ponder over one of my thoughts, "how many real friends do we really have that walk this journey with us on this earth?"

As men, we like to hold back our thoughts and feelings for the most part. The holding back makes it more difficult to open up because, over the years, we have silenced our inside voices. We feel like opening up to another man is a form of weakness. As men, we want to act like we always have our act together. We want to act tough. This is the very reason why we have so many men who feel lonely and isolated. We do face challenges with how to best express our thoughts and feelings.

'The first mountain we have to overcome is the importance of sharing and expressing our thoughts and feelings.'

We tend to feel like if we ignore our inner voice, we will be okay. I know and understand we must be very careful who we share our thoughts and feelings with. Our inner thoughts and feelings are at the very core of who we are and our internal settings.

As Men, we have friends in different categories.

On Level Three are ideal friends. On Level Two would be utility friends, something you like about that person. At level One will be well-being.

These are the friends at the highest level; there is a spiritual connection and a social connection that draws out one's bounding too. Two of My real true friends, under the well-being level ONE, would be my brothers Gowi and Emmanuel. It's with these two friends that I open up my heart and share my inner thoughts. Over the past twelve years with my friend Gowi, I have been able to open up about my challenges and struggles. I feel relaxed around Gowi, and I am able to just be myself. I enjoy his companionship as we just have simple moments with a lot of laughter. I do not feel any form of judgment begin past during our time together which makes me open up and be real. We continue to grow together on our spiritual journey as iron sharpens iron.

I also have another great true friend Emmanuel. We have grown up together and have known each other for over 40 years. I'm currently 52 years old as I finish my book. We played so many fun games together in primary school and high school. We have played marbles together for days on end and sometimes even skipped class just to play for marbles. We have done many cheeky things together over the numerous years. We did crazy things together and got into many bar fights during our drunken days. We have both enjoyed the bottle and the ladies in our thirties especially, as we lived an aimless, reckless life. We even enjoy watching cartoons together. Emmanuel's favorite cartoon is Pink Panther, and my favorite is Tom and Jerry. Sometimes, we just look at each other and start laughing for no reason at all.

My friend Emmanuel turned his life over to Christ in the year 2006. He has been a born-again Christian since then. He is a happily married man with three young boys.

My friend Emmanuel and I pray together a lot. We discuss our different prayers, we discuss our different dreams, and We encourage each other. Emmanuel is gifted with blazing love to share the word of God in our Good Bible. I really enjoy beginning around Emmanuel and just enjoying the simple moments in life.

However, over the last three years, Emmanuel and I have become a bit distant. And A big part of the pullback on my part is connected to his myopic vision of Rwanda. Emmanuel is able to point out the shortcomings of our Kenyan President and other political discussions we have from time to time. However, the thought of even discussing the shortcomings of the Rwandan President or political atmosphere is a No-No.

'This method of looking the other way is a cancer building up in Rwanda under an oppressive dictator, the President of Rwanda's Paul Kagame rule of law.'

The tension fills up the room at the thought of trying to give one's opinion. The rule of law is only to be viewed as Kagame's law. No one should say anything different or have different opinions. On my end, I speak with authority as I have seen and witnessed firsthand the ways of my tormentors by Rwandan authorities. The art of covering the truth is done with total perfection.

I view Rwanda now differently, having fallen in love with Rwanda, having fled from Rwanda, and having experienced threats on my life from Rwanda. I have close family members and so-called friends who try and advise me not to publish this book, driven by fear of what will happen to me.

'I am shining my light on the truth that has been kept in darkness from this tiny nation, Rwanda. The other side of the coin.'

Yes, the threat over the phone from Rwandan authorities was chilling into my bones.

The words are so clear today, even after over eleven years on:

"We will place your body where flies will never find you."

My friend Emmanuel has either become blinded or has decided to look the other way as his method of avoiding the truth. We have far different views of Rwanda.

'I have lived to see the fangs of death firsthand.'

Emmanuel decided to just look the other way to find his own peace through avoidance. This is the cause of my strained relationship with one of my best friends, Emmanuel.

"I AM DONE"

I remember very clearly sitting with a few friends on December 30th, 2011, having a few beers. I was at a friend's house in Karen with a few ladies and lots of alcohol. My world actually paused in slow motion as I looked around each table in slow motion at everyone's faces.

'Then a voice spoke to my heart, "Nathan is this what I created you for?" I knew right there God was disappointed in me and how I was living my life.' I had just given my life to Christ a few weeks ago, in August 2011, with no change in how I lived. On The night of December 30th, 2011, I stood up and placed my beer on the table, and said to everyone in a loud voice, "I AM DONE." This sealed the night in which my actions matched giving my life to Jesus Christ.

'I was truly born-again in Mind and Spirit.'

I had made the U-Turn of my life. My life belonged to God and God alone.

I was really DONE. In fact, on December 30th, 2022, we marked Eleven Years as a born-again Christian and Alcohol-free.

'Re-Cap'

During all of my thirties, I lived and worked in Rwanda. I got married to a Rwandan wife Cleophase Kabaasita at the age of thirty-two years. We had been Blessed with two wonderful kids named Darrel and Crystal. Darrel was born in the USA in February 2002, and Crystal was born in Rwanda in July 2003.

'Born Again Challenges Triple'

As I look back over the years, it's Interesting as we tend to think that once one is born again, there are no more challenges. In my own personal experiences, the challenges doubled and tripled after I gave my life to Christ. As I let go fully in December 2011 to allow God to come into my life, at the very same time, the devil also decided to try and push me back to my old ways.

'My earthly world had blown up exactly like a volcano.'

I was on the run from my former foreign home, Rwanda. Those who had been my friends turned into foes, and my wife then called it quits on our marriage and took my two kids to America against my will. To add insult to injury, my former wife Cleophase Kabasiita turned against me too and joined the critics. My Dad's health started failing, and he passed away in August 2012. I stood with my dad and offered all my financial and emotional support with a roof over his head. I did support my father fully even during my darkest days. After I fled Rwanda I lived with my Dad in Nairobi in an expensive apartment I bought in the year 2009. I let my Dad have the master bedroom and gave him all the African respect.

'My Blessings continue today because I also kept the respect and supported my father, Owen Ndungu, even when my life was upside down.'

Cleophase pushed me with conditions, to make a decision, to kick my ailing father out of my apartment, if I wanted her to return. I could not and did not.

'Gaping Hole'

Overview, I was on the run as a fugitive, with no funds, no wife, and no kids, with a gaping hole of emptiness in my heart. I remember crying several times at night, asking God, is this what being born again feels like? It sure did not feel like this was worth it at all. I would ponder, thinking about my old days of consuming alcohol; at least for about seven hours twice a week, I would forget my pains. I would be so intoxicated that

I felt free for a few hours from worry. I got lost in another world that made me feel like my problems were not bad at all. I was able to put my head on the ground and forget about the world above.

Successful Failures Lesson Take Away:

'Over the years, I came to realize, once we are born again, it does not mean that we start to float on a smooth cloud. I must admit I still face challenges over eleven years down my journey after giving my life to Christ. The biggest difference, and the Whole difference, is Now My God is with me. Yes, the challenges do come, and I handle my part and let My Father, My God, handle what I am unable to handle. God created me, so he knows best how to handle the parts I am unable to handle.'

This is also why I am sure of this:

" I am Not yet the Man I want to Be, but I am sure Not the Man I used to Be."

CHAPTER 8 – BLOCKED MINDS

Description: +1%

One of the current thoughts that comes to mind today is, why do we block our minds and switch our minds off? We do so to the point that we are not able to see our faults or our shortcomings. We have become professionals over the weeks, months, and years on end to avoid seeing our blind spots. *'We sometimes even become defensive when a real call out on our blind spot is pointed out.'*

As I ponder over this, it makes me think more about why we really do not want to know ourselves better and understand our weaknesses.

'Once we know our weaknesses, we become stronger and better, and this yields a better life here on earth.'

Sometimes along the road of life, we get frustrated, and we turn to blame the world around us, yet we are the cause.

'Our experiences come from within, and we have the liberty to learn from them if we want to'.

We have control of our minds and our thoughts; this builds into the direction we take in life through our daily habits.

If you really want change, change the little part called habits for a positive direction. Once you take time to study yourself, you will learn what needs to change to achieve what you need to achieve in life.

'Our habits are powerful, and worth understanding that this small daily change will yield huge positive results'.

One of the key parts here is we must slow down, understand ourselves, spend time with ourselves, and enjoy being around ourselves. I say this from my own experiences in life.

How does one get to know themselves daily?

It's simply spending quality time with yourself every day or at least five days a week as a minimum. Friends, it only takes sixty minutes a day to have quality time that springboards your morning before daybreak. It's a must that during this time, you stay away from any gadgets and away from any TV.

'It is very important to isolate yourself and be by yourself to get to know yourself daily. Our betterment comes from within, not from the outside world'.

I can tell you for a fact that if I spend 99% of my first walking hour with No phone, No gadget, No TV, No tablet, and No other electronic device at all. If I have to travel and, for some reason, wake up later than 5 am, I will still make sure my one solid hour remains untouched. These first 60 minutes a day will direct your life into a guaranteed better, clear life here on earth. If that was all you did for that day, your day would still be a well-spent day.

'5am Club'

Looking at one of the books that I've read, called "The 5 am Club" by Robin Sharma, highlights the power of this hour. This book covers the value and importance of segmenting your first hour, the 5 am, into 20 minutes, 20 minutes, and 20 minutes. Divide this power hour into three short, powerful sections of 20 minutes. The first 20 minutes are focused on a form of exercise that gets your heart racing. Then the next 20 minutes are a time of reflection, a time for prayer with yourself. In this stillness, prayer time, and communication time, you get to listen to God's voice. Use the last 20 minutes to wrap up the hour for growth with simple plans of action.

'It's through these small power bits that we divide our time into physical growth, spiritual growth, and directional growth'.

This happens even before the world has woken up, the first Golden hour that builds on the rocks of a Golden life. Imagine one Golden hour a day, taking us through five days of the week. This gives us Five solid Golden hours in one week alone. Let's take fifty weeks for the year. Yes, that means in one year alone, one will have achieved 250 hours of Positive, Physical, Spiritual and Directional growth. Let's keep in mind these 250 hours over the year have each hour controlled your day settings ahead of the daybreak.

'Our Victories are achieved before the day starts; this gives us better control of the day beforehand'.

During my Golden hour, I don't see any other human being, neither my kids nor my wife.

'It's during this romantic time I get to grow as I get to develop myself, putting me in a better place to handle the day before the day starts.'

I really don't understand why people let the day control them and wonder why they get so worked up and confused.

'You and you alone can control your day by giving that time to the most important person on this earth, yourself.'

We tend to sometimes think through blocking our minds, all looks fine, and all checks out. One of the reasons why we do that is to try and make ourselves look better or feel better. We don't want to see or face our shortcomings and prefer to hide away from ourselves daily.

'It's only through seeing our shortcomings that we will realize where we need to improve.'

Once we realize where we need to improve, we get better and better at growing ourselves.

"We tend to shy away from seeing our faults, yet this is the only way to grow oneself."

I've also said several times to my family members and friends:

'Without change, there can be no change." It sounds so simple because it is simple. Without change, there can be no Change.'

'Change within'

I get so amazed as we cross into a new year when I hear people declare their New Year's resolutions. I hear them saying this is the year of change. I was one of those people myself about ten years ago. I see and hear Pastors/Fathers from different churches jumping up and down with joy that this is your year. This year favor and change are coming your way. This joy and feeling of new hope fades away as the year goes mid-way past, and towards the end of the same year, you release no change.

'The reason nothing changes even after men of the cloth say they have Prayed about it and change is coming is that you have not changed your ways.'

The disappointing part is that year after year, there is no change until you realize you need to change your ways and habits. Because without change, there can be no change.

'Atomic Habits are Major'

This directs my thoughts to another great book I read called *'Atomic Habits.'* The focus was on how small, minor, and little changes do change our outcomes. Reference was made to an ice cube. When we place an ice cube on the table and the temperature is at 25 degrees, it does not melt. As the temperature goes up to 26, 27, 28, and 29 degrees, going up 1% at a time, nothing happens. We see no change, and all looks the same. It's during this time of the 1% increase that it all looks like it makes no difference, and one gives up. The small unseen changes are taking place unseen to the naked eye. As the temperature continues to rise up to 30 and 31 degrees yet the ice cube on the table still shows no signs of visual change. The change is taking place at such a small level unseen to the naked eye still. However, small changes are taking place. When we get to 32 degrees, the ice cube starts to melt, and this we can see with our eyes.

The key part is that a very small charge was taking place within, but we could not yet see it on the outside. The lesson learned is that unseen change was taking place between 25 degrees and 31 degrees. This is always a very important time that takes a lot of effort and alot of faith. Sadly, this is the time most of us give up. It's at the 32-degree mark; we tend to say all of a sudden this and this happened. The reality in life is that nothing is all of a sudden in this world.

'It's all about what we do not see, the dark hours, the long nights, and the tears of pain turned into tears of joy'.

We sometimes hear in the news or different people saying that all of a sudden, this or that happened. It's simple; it's a simple, steady +1% change every single day that will melt the ice cube every time. Melting the ice cube is the overall reference to life.

'The small minor change in our habits may be unseen, but these minor changes flow into the desired results one step at a time'.

During that time, change is taking place, but we don't notice; we tend to say and feel like it makes no difference, so we give up. The little baby steps, the little change makes a world of difference within the +1% daily. We change our 1% by changing our habits.

'When it comes to looking at positive habits, look at them from the end result that you so desire.'

Ask yourself the hard questions. What do I want to achieve within my goals?

'As you go about changing your daily 1%, keep the end goal in mind.'

Let's say, in the case of weight loss; you have to have a positive image of how you would like to look over a specific desired timeline.

Imagine how you would like to look in one month or two months, or three months. Keep the short-term goals as your key focus within a short period of time. Then once achieved, set a new set of short-term goals. This push keeps your mind focused on the end results.

'When it comes to how to start correcting negative habits, think of the negative results you are getting or will get without change.'

An example of that would be, "I would like to stop smoking because this will change the way my lips look as they are turning black." So, if I stop, I will start my journey to a better image of myself and better health for myself." Yes, this process does take time and willpower, along with the small daily changes.

'The results always pay off, and this is your life, so take care of yourself. Be the change you want to see'.

Thoughts to self:

***

"The ones who take the road of least resistance are the ones who usually are quick to judge."

"The non-starters, the dreams without action, are always first online to pass judgment."

Famous words used by 'non-starters' who are usually haters: "If it was me, I would have done it this way or that way." They have become experts from the sidelines of life and professional criticism.

Successful Failures Lesson Take Away:

"*Sometimes in life, we have to do what we don't want to do to get what we eventually want to get.*"

"*This is yet another feather on my hat within 'My Successful Failures' learning the Lesson.*"

My Successful Failures

CHAPTER 9 – FLOCK TOGETHER

<u>Description: Mental Detector</u>

As I remember back in the day, in high school, we used to be told that birds of a feather flock together. I used to brush this off as nonsense. When I come to think about it now as an adult, it is very true. The people you associate with or hang around with are the ones you'll most likely end up being like.

'Once you show me the five people you spend most of your time with, it is a true reflection of who you are, positive or negative.'

I no longer brush off the saying, birds of a feather flock together, for I know this is spot on. The people you associate with or spend most of your time with are what you become.

As we move through life and during those pause moments, we feel we want to change a few areas in our life for our own betterment. You want to set a new path on this journey we call life.

'This change or improvement of direction on your spiritual journey, your business, or your personal new path needs changing your flock.'

What's going to have to change are the people around you; you will have to get a new flock for the ones who do not add value to your life.

'During those special times alone, take time to think and study yourself and those around you.'

It will come to light and clearly show that those who contribute to a better you are the keepers, and those that do not, you need to pull away. The flock that is not for you are the ones who are not contributing to your growth and development.

Think about the five different people you spend the most time with for five minutes each. Then ask yourself once I am done spending my time together with that specific person. How do I really feel? "Do I feel rejuvenated," or "Do I feel energized?" Or "Do I feel poisoned?" or "Do I feel a sense of bitterness? These top five people you spend most of your time with are directing your life as you both interact. Based on different forms of advice during one's time together, set your train of thought.

The advantage of the five people you spend most of your time with is you get a fair balance of different views. Over time as one matures and develops wisdom, you get to know who is there to build you and who is there to try and destroy you. Once you know who is for you and is supporting you to build the character you want, these are keepers. On the other hand, those who offer advice that does not feel right based on who you are or who you want to be, are weeds.

'Weeds are exactly like the weeds we have in our gardens. Weeds take our energy, Weeds block our growth, and over time weeds destroy and kill us.'

We can have so-called friends that will push to try and get us to focus on revenge, revenge, yet revenge is not for us to do revenge. Let God do what God has to do in the way only God knows. Our part is telling the truth and keeping it truthful; the rest is for God. If you want to become a better person than the person that you currently are, you must diligently look at the five people around you. It's sad that some of your flock will have to go for the betterment of who you want to become. The key to note is that this is your life, and we only live life once. Become alert and Become aware of those around you to support and achieve the you that you are on the inside.

'Foolish Advice'

The old saying, *'you can't teach an old dog new tricks,'* is rubbish. This really comes from the mouths of people who have given up on life. They refuse to change their within to get new better conditions in their without. In turn, they stay the same, and fear takes the day.

This same foolish advice is repeated several times by one of my former close friends Edwin George Muturi. The reference of one cannot teach an old dog new tricks reflects useless advice mixed in with a give up mentality. On one hand is the reference of a human being compared to a dog. On the other hand life is not about tricks but about daily growth.

'Interestingly enough what comes from one's mouth is a reflection on how one's tomorrow will look.'

In the example of Edwin Muturi his life has remained the same with no difference for the past thirty five years that I have known him.

When I ask Edwin, is he not concerned about remaining with no value added to make this world a better place.

'Edwins, response is that it is fate.'

Sadly his shallow thinking has yielded his life. This is why Edwin is not part of my new flock for the past well over twelve years. Edwins, give up mentality and blaming the world at large has caused him to miss out on living a life filled with purpose. A really sad flat way to live life, I see in my former Friend Edwin Muturi.

'Mental Detectors.'

When we are set to travel by air, we go to the airport and come to the security checkpoint. It's at this security checkpoint that we go through metal detectors to make sure that everything that we carry is safe and allowed onto the Airplane. If, for some reason, this is not safe, we are requested to remove the item or items that will not be allowed onto the plane. In this same manner, we need to switch on our mental detectors as an alert to our minds.

'In this way, allow only what you feel will enrich you and build you into making you a better person. This is one of the methods I have used and continue to use every single day, and it builds my internal peace.'

My mental detectors are also dependent on who I'm sitting around. People who are hurting and people who are jealous want desperately to pass this venom into you, so you join them on their bitter journey. Be very careful who advises you and from what area of experience the said person is coming.

'Keeping in mind those who know the least about life tend to act and pretend like they know it all.'

These are very dangerous people to be around, for they speak like they have experience with everything. Yet, they have very little or no experience with the topic at hand but want to look intellectual.

'Warning Danger.'

A lot of times, the advice is coming to try and activate the unwanted results. The advice is coming from a place that is unbalanced with no merit to add any value. Sometimes you will get advice from people who are jealous of you, people who are envious of you, and people who are not happy to see you're excelling in your different areas of life. The level of tried cleverness is well masked to try and make it look like it comes from a place of Love. The words used will be emotional words like I am your family, brother, brother in -law, sister or I am your blood.

'These words will be used to open the gate into your heart for the attack to take place.'

Once you open your heart up, the person has "free will" to walk around your heart and destroy you.

'All in the fake aim of love that is really coming from a place of hate.'

The aim is to bring you down to their level or below their level to make them look better and feel better.

When you seek advice, there is nothing wrong with having specific criteria and listening to different opinions. On my end, before I seek advice, I need to know and find out more about the person and what they do. For example, if somebody has to offer me marital advice, they'll have to be married, with children, and must be a believer. Even if it's a pastor offering advice that does not fit my three criteria rule. In this situation on Religion, Married, and having kids. I have to respectfully decline to listen to them, for they are coming from a place that is unknown to them. If for whatever reason, I find myself in an awkward position where they have decided to impose themselves; I just switch on my mental detector. I am surprised that a lot of people from all walks of life try and advise me on business, yet they have no business experience at all.

'Keep alert; keep in tune on who is speaking or trying to speak into your life. It's very important to shy away and distance yourself from those who add no value at all.'

'Expensive Coffee, Why ?'

Once a good friend of mine asked me, how come you go to expensive places for a nice cup of coffee?

'My response: "Our surroundings determine our thought process.'

If you want to think big, go to big places to think, and vice versa. Once you change your surroundings and change those people that add no value to your life, then your life will change for the better.

'In order to dream big and make your blood flow with excitement, change your environment.'

Once you start dreaming big, you need to act big. This has nothing to do with acting prideful at all. Then, once the dream is in hand, take baby steps forward. I call the baby steps every day the PLUS ONE (+1%) daily and keep moving; do not stop. Yes, failure will come and does come. However this is success in the making as you get better and better with the +1% daily moving towards your goals.

Thought to self:

***

"If the Man fails, he hands over leadership, his shield, and his spear to the Wife."

Successful Failures Lesson Take Away:

It is in the journey that we find growth, not in sitting back and talking about what we would have or could have been able to do. My current surroundings, mixed with years of failing, with years of being called names, have propelled me into a World Seasoned, tested Super Leader and Great Mentor.

MR. NATHAN LOYD

CHAPTER 10 - WITHINS

Description: Growth is Inward.

'The Rot Within'

Even after my escape for my life, from Rwanda in 2011, my tormentors continued. My properties have all been taken by the Rwandan authorities, and my bank accounts have been frozen by the very same country that caused the problem. This is what happens in Rwanda: point the finger, play the victim and act by illegally taking people's property as a form of correction.

'It's worse, the authorities justify their actions as legal and fair. So deeply rooted in the rot of lies that the same people in Rwanda have come to believe their own lies as truths.'

My ordeal continues as I push to finish my book within the latest attempt on my life, in January 2022. This attempt on my life was planned in cahoots with my ex-Rwandese wife, Cleophase Kabaasita, feeding information to Rwandan authorities. In turn, our Kenyan police acted like puppets. The evil plan was to get me off the plane on landing at JKIA Nairobi and kidnap me onto a plane to Rwanda for my demise.

Let's take a step back the Rwandese authorities caused the legislative mortgage law shift and then so it fit to find a crime to charge me with. In the purported criminal offense, I was tried and found guilty in absentia and sentenced to five years in prison to serve in Rwanda in 2012. Let's keep one fact in mind no where in the World can one be tried for a criminal offense in absentia.

'In a nutshell, cause the problem and then play the victim as a form of justification. The real question comes back to who made the mistake after all. Who is the real criminal?'

'Spain 55 Days in Hell'

This has dogged my life from 2011 to ongoing 2022 as I am labeled a so-called fugitive. I was tormented and arrested in Spain and held for fifty-five days under country arrest in 2018. After fifty days under country arrest in Spain in 2018, all charges were dropped.

'Dubai 75 Days in Hell'

I was then arrested in Dubai and held under country arrest for seventy-five days in 2021. After seventy-five days, the same case was dismissed. My name has been dragged through the mud for the past twelve years, all with the aim of covering the real villain.

'Kenya 90 Days in Hell'

The same nightmare took place for the third time on my arrival in Nairobi in January 2022. I was arrested and held in a cell for eight days. Then an additional seventy two days of having to hide from the illegal attempts of DCI in Kenya. The authorities in Kenya, in cohorts with Rwandeses tormentors tried everything possible to kidnap me illegally and take me to Rwanda. This marked ninety days. The Rwandan authorities did what they do best, they built up lies on lies that they are tough on corruption.

The question really is who is really corrupt when from the top the Rwandan President Paul Kagame lives a life of deception for self-gain. Paul Kagame has perfected the art of cover up to try and show he is not corrupt with a totally clean cover up image to the world at large.

One little issue was overlooked by the Rwandan side.

"I AM a protected child of My God."

Over the last twelve years, I've been threatened to keep silent and not give my side of the story of what happened and what went wrong. It's a very normal practice in Rwanda to focus on their image of perfection and play the victim at any cost. I do mean at any cost at all.

This is the very reason Rwanda is ranked as one of the worst countries in the world due to human rights violations. Rwanda has perfected the art of deception and being able to fool the world at large for the most part.

'Fake Red Alert'

In my case, Rwandan authorities provided misleading information to Interpol, and this activated the Red Alert notice to hunt me down. The aim was twofold: one; I was offered to bribe a very high official in the Rwandan Government, and two, to keep hunting me down. As a born-again Christian, I refused to pay this bribe in 2012. Thus, their commitment is to keep tainting my image and falsify documents to purport that I was found guilty.

'How can I be found guilty in Rwanda, when the whole court and judicial system is controlled by one person. Yes, you guessed it, dictator President Paul Kagame.'

Image this I am placed on Rwanda's most wanted next to genocide suspects with their top ten most wanted. I have been hunted down like a genocide suspect, like a murderer, like a drug dealer for over twelve years.

'I feel saddened that my own birth country Kenya believed the lies drummed up in Rwanda over a decade ago.'

My home, My Motherland, My place of birth would actually turn the other way, with our Kenyan media in tow to call me a fugitive. Added to the attempt to have me illegally kidnapped and placed on a plane to Rwanda to face the end of my life based on false claims.

'Now let's take a pause.'

Kenya has no valid extradition agreement with Rwanda. The civil debt was paid off in August 2012. One simple question: what is this really all about to face nothing or another sinister motive? The signed settlement agreement was kept away from Interpol to make the fake crime seem still active.

'What a sad state of a country, Rwanda, that builds its reputation on lies upon lies.'

The settlement agreement was signed in Rwanda by none other than the Minister of Justice himself in August 2012. I wonder who made sure my company debt was paid off by selling my other properties. Guess who it was? It was 'Me.' I got the investors to pay off my company debt in full 100% in the year 2012.

'To allow the Rwandan government to look like heroes, they made it look like they found the investors. What a far cry from the truth.'

It's all on the official file, my recorded and written statements that I'm concerned for my life. The Rwandan authorities are using the Kenyan authorities as puppets.

'In Kenya, we face major issues like terrorism, and yet they are fooled into going blindly after one of their very own Kenyan blood brothers.'

I tell you this if the tables had been turned to go after another Rwandan and use the Rwandan police for the rubbish, they would not move an inch.

The trigger goes back to my ex-wife Cleophase Kabasiita, who, for over a decade, has tried everything possible to have me eliminated and fanned the flame.

'Keep in mind she is now a US citizen living in my country as she acts on her deceitful attempts.'

As she sits back and watches her former husband hunted down like a wild animal. The state of her heart of deep, deep devil deeds.

It's suspicious how Cleophase Kabasiita became a US citizen in my country and went on even further to take my last name 'Loyd'. This too is being looked into as her lies are about to catch up to her deceitful games.

'Blood Punches'

I was at the bottom of the bottom in 2011, added in I lost my father in 2012. In addition it was at this time, at the turn of 2013, that my wife Cleophase then took on the fight to the Kenyan courts to try and take away my two wonderful kids. This was a legal battle that took place in the Kenyan children's court.

'Picture This'

In October 2011, I fled for my life; IN February 2012, I was placed on Interpol and added to that, my father passed away IN August 2012. As we stepped into 2013, during my ongoing lowest moments, still as my wife, Cleophase tried to fight to have my kids taken away from me. In her court filings for my kids' custody, ninety percent of the documents her lawyer submitted had the focus on 'Interpol' looking for me. Cleophase had put together all the drummed-up charges against me to present as evidence.

'So picture this Cleophase tried everything possible to have me destroyed and killed.'

Cleophase had taken me to children's court over our kids' custody as an additional level to try and destroy me. Added in was her focus on how to have me arrested and extradited to Rwanda to be eliminated.

'The Ruling is in'

As the female Judge stated before her final ruling, "***What do Interpol issues have to do in a children's court.***" The ruling was I, Daddy/ Father was the better-fit parent to raise my son Darrel and Crystal. I fought the good fight with a brave heart for my kids. I was able to bring them up, even when my life was upside down and my tormentors on my heels.

'As my Father in Heaven fights for His children, so did I fight for my kids.'

I was hit with spears into my back as pure blood of pain dripped from my invisible wounds for over a decade. I faced the world head on as the king leader I became with the pure courage to say this. I am very Okay and was able to fight for my young family as a whole deceitful country came to try & destroy me. Rwanda, a whole country, had to face the great man I had grown into with my victorious God as my shield and protector.

IF YOU WANT TO BE SUCCESSFUL, FACE YOUR FEARS BECAUSE A KING IS NOT BORN, HE IS MADE. WORK HARD

This is one of my greatest joys today when I look back at the many dark nights. The simple, pure messages from my kids with loving thanks for shielding and protecting them during their childhood days. My ex-wife tried to convince me several times I should just be a holiday father over the years.

I would ponder deeply if my Father in Heaven is a Holiday Father. No He is not. My God is an active supporting, Loving Father. As a born again Christian I walked deeply in His footsteps through many valleys and onto the hilltops. I have shouted several times Hallelujah Hallelujah !!!!!

"I was a solid, firm, brave father as my father in Heaven is."

My son Darrel is now a young, strong adult man in his junior year in college in the US. My young beautiful adult daughter Crystal is a sophomore in college in the US. What peaceful joy each of my precious kids have told me at different times:

"Daddy, Thank You for fighting for us with every breath that you had."

As a man and a father, there were easy ways to just give up and take the easy way out of giving up.

'I fought to grow up with my kids, through the tears and through the dark nights.'

It's true I lost all my material possessions in Rwanda and my old friends turned to be my new enemies. My foes tried everything possible to finish me and bury me.

'However, when I gave my life to Jesus Christ in December 2011, I got my soul back.'

'In my mind, I now know with God for me who can be against me.'

I am not saying in any way that I did not and have not faced challenges in my life as a born-again Christian. The difference is I now know God is beside me, fighting with me and protecting me with His shield. I enjoy spending a lot of quiet time with my maker in the early morning hours, before day break.

It's through these special moments I've grown into a Better, Stronger, Wiser man through God's Grace in my life.

Successful Failures Lesson Take Away:

'It's breathtaking to feel God's gentle voice through the morning breeze on my ears and cheeks. During these numerous moments it's just my God and me. My heart melts with pure joy as my eyes fill with tears of joy feeling God touching my soul'.

'Victory belongs to God and God alone.'

CHAPTER 11 - HIGH ROAD

Description: 'Protected Most High'.

In early May 2022, one quiet morning over a cup of coffee. I was pondering about the value of taking the high road when my reputation and kind nature have been taken advantage of for several years and ongoing. This I ponder deeply as my ex-Rwandese wife Cleophase Kabaasita continues to plot for my death through her deceitful means with her malice lies. The plot is to have me eliminated as she feeds information to my enemies to find my whereabouts for nothing at all but settle for nothing with the aim of making herself look good.

'Twelve years in Camouflage.'

This comes from the nature of who Cleophase is, a born trained lier and she remained well camouflaged during the twelve years we had been married. I mean camouflaged because I never did see this side of hers over the twelve years we had been married. Love this time around was really blind. My Ex-Rwandese wife Cleophase continues to be spiteful and to literally throw me under the bus steaming from a purported civil legal issue in Rwanda.

'Add to the facts that Cleophase was never a faithful wife & had several sexual affairs during the time we had been married with top officials within the Rwandan Government.

It's some of these very same Rwandese officials she had sexual affairs with that she calls onto to find me & destroy me. To be clear is to find me & have me killed.

Rwandese Authorities working with Cleophase, who is also Rwandese, have been able to turn a civil offense into a criminal offense. This is notorious for what Rwandese high officials do very well to hundreds of people for the last two decades.

'The true masters of deception comes from the very top, the President of Rwanda Paul Kagame with his puppets.'

Sadly a few of these people have been whipped off the face of this earth never to tell their side.

'As a Christian and as a believer, I told myself that I would state the facts to the American authorities, which I have done. **Enough is Enough !!!** '

'My life has been threatened for too long enough.'

An element of anger seeps into me as this challenges my soul. I feel burning up within me the need for revenge to settle the score. The battle rages on with the two voices in my head; one says flight, and the other says this is not your battle to fight. On the one hand, how can this not be my battle to fight? It's my life at stake here on earth. On the other hand, I am reminded that I am a Christian man that depends on God alone. This means I Pray about it and do my part of telling the truth and allow God to do His part.

'Country = Culture'

Once one gets to understand the overall culture of upbringing in any country, one gets to better understand key parts about the person. In the case of Rwanda, a country notoriously known for masking and hiding the truth is where my Ex-Wife, Cleophase grew up.

"Have you noticed"

Have you noticed when you check into a hotel, they let you know the breakfast start time and end time.? On my end, I pay keen attention to the start time as my wife and kids focus on the end time.

I look in wonder from the side lounge, after a wonderful full hour of Breakfast. As I sip on my nice cappuccino enjoying the morning breeze & looking at the ocean waves. I see these last minute guests of the hotel dashing all over the breakfast buffet to place as much food on their dish. Now, imagine this is done during the last ten minutes before breakfast is over. Then I watch a few of them get so worked up as they complain about why breakfast ends so soon.

'Sweet Spot'

On my end, I get to enjoy the sweet spot, the fresh start, and the morning fresh morning scent of coffee & eggs. These sweet, simple moments are part of what makes life so beautiful. No rush as I walk towards the breakfast lounge with slippers on in a slow slow-motion chilled walk. The glow on my face from enjoying the simple moments with fresh Good Mornings.

'This gives me an opportunity to enjoy the simple and reconnect to my soul.

Have you noticed in life, in business, that an early start, an early planning, and an early quiet time every morning are key to one's growth and success?

'We grow mentally and spiritually only when we have 'Me Time',' or 'Alone Time'.'

Have you noticed only those who spend quiet time alone, before day break, have changed the world and rule the world?

'In-built By God.'

The ones that take time to disconnect and go within to find the power within. It's so clear in the Bible, we are created in His image.

'In His image means the powers are in-built within. '

We are only able to tap into our core with a continuous process of finding ourselves.

Get to spend time with the person that matters most to you, yourself. It's a great feeling to keep falling in love with yourself. I see so many people, family, and friends that will do anything not to spend time alone. The focus is on their phones, on the television, checking in on social events, and checking in on what people are saying about them.

'It's only during this power victory hour that one reconnects to connect and grow.'

Thoughts to Self:

Families, frenemies, and enemies are quick to judge others, yet do so out of jealousy.

- A dreamer needs to be a doer, as dreams without daily small daily steps are just dead dreams.

- Manageable Manageability is also shown in how one deals with a problem or a challenge at hand, mentally.

- The outlook at the end of the day comes from how one has handled the inward process.

Thoughts to Self:

"Things will change when you change."

"Humility with confidence."

"The spirit of courage, the warrior, the king, I became."

"Feel the fear and do it anyway."

"In the darkness, the silence we find – growth."

Successful Failures Lesson Take Away:

Take time to study, the person, the country & take time to dig deeper before getting married to the person or the country. In this way you get to know the roots of the person & the country before making a move.

I did not do this ahead only to find out the real Cleophase with her deceitful nature & the real Rwanda filled with notorious lies built in as truths.

CHAPTER 12 - WISDOM YEARS

Description: Balanced Insights.

"Who walked in the door with you?"

Today, I re-learned that in business; a no is only a delayed yes. As a businessman, this must never define who you are but only build you as you turn into who you are going to be. We are who we turn out to be based on how we look at the big word 'NO.' I said 'No,' 'No,' and 'No,' and looked at this no, no, and no as a delay to come yes, yes, and yes.

'I have walked through life; I have tested the fire and the heat and felt the bottom.'

As I look back today at the age of forty-eight, I smile. Why? Because the journey, the fire, and the bottom have molded me into a solid gold person of great reputation.

'Ladies and gentlemen, depending on who you walk into the possible deal with, can predetermine the closing of the deal or not'

I enjoy matchmaking deals, the thrill of what looks impossible to most. This is where the honey is, deep inside the honeycomb.

If you do walk into a possible deal with the wrong person it can be a deal breaker for you. Take a step back and assess the deal and make sure you are with the right person to support you in closing the deal on the table.

A case in point this past week, I was matchmaking a deal connected to Ethiopia. I walked into the meeting with who I thought was the right person, only to learn the very person presented false facts, which to him were true facts. So yes, the meeting turned out to be not Interested in the deal on the table.

'One of the biggest dangerous challenges we face in life is people pretending to know what they do not know. '

'An expert in everything and anything, avoid these people at all costs.'

It's fine if you end up having a cup of coffee together, laugh and smile but switch off the listening ear.

Fast-forward a week later, same deal, different person. This time around, the facts ran out to be better placed, and our deal was successful. Lesson learned, always do your homework on the person you think will support you to close the deal. In the same cases, you can close the deal alone and could have better chances.

'The spirit, the resilience, the go-getter attitude, the persistence has built my solid foundation for success on success. We continue, we challenge, we fight, and we grow through hard times to shine into the stars we become.'

"What does persistence mean?"

In this race called life, we must know that to make changes; one must undergo changes from within. The changes and the blows are big and painful, but if you keep with persistence, you will feel the gain. When and if we learn from what looks like failure to the naked eye, then we grow.

'Ladies and gentlemen, real growth only comes from one's successful failures.'

These successful failures are only achieved by learning from experience, the lesson. We grow from learning the lesson and moving forward daily. This comes from persistence. Never give up, even when friends and family members do their very best to try and have you give up on your own dreams.

'Remember, sometimes you win, and sometimes you learn. We never lose if we learn the lesson.'

My advice is to enjoy learning. Enjoy pushing forward and avoid those who have given up. If you do not like your job, create your job. I am totally amazed when I hear people say that they get a job for security. The critical flaw here is, are they successful because they have a job, or is the true success of the one who created the job?

'Real job security comes from creating your own job.'

Look back over the last 200 years and find one person that had a job and, through the job, gained notoriety. The movers and shakers of this world owned up and found their calling and, in turn, changed the world. The other ninety percent of the population fell into fear and claimed job security as their path. A key difference between the doers is persistence and going through the pain to enjoy the gain: Freedom!

Feeding our minds.

Take time to check daily what you are really feeding your mind as your within will turn out to be your without. I check daily, especially first thing in the morning, my food of thought to keep building who I am becoming daily.

'As you are doing so, always keep your mental detectors switched on.'

As your thoughts and plans stream in for the day, focus on action, and items that will build you. The none energy-draining items must be deleted; done with! These are weeds to drain your energy and add no value.

As I mentioned before, we have metal detectors at airports to make sure we do not carry anything dangerous into the planes.

'We too must have our mental detectors on to make sure we do not carry anything dangerous into our minds.'

These negative thoughts, many times, will be supported by friends and family. Since they have either switched off their mental detectors or do not know how to switch their detectors on, they would like you to join them. Take off the breaks and go for it, for your gift is already in you.

Mental Detector.

Friends, daily, keep your mental detector switched on to block out the negative and grow the positive.

'The negative thoughts come to steal your joy, steal the lesson, steal the peace, and plant weeds.'

As you keep your detector on, pull out the weeds, retain the peace, retain the joy and enjoy the moments of joy. In turn, positivity will build on positivity. The negative thoughts will come, but with a switched-on detector, the weeds will not grow.

We take note of the following:

"Do not be comforted by this world, but be transformed by the renewing of your mind that you may prove what is good and acceptable and perfect Will of God" Romans 12:2."

The renewing of your mind daily, not what people say about you, but what you say and think about yourself.

'Friends, stop being concerned about what people say about you; it is none of your business!'

Focus on you, the renewing of your mind daily.

'We are each created in His image; is that not a Wonderful Feeling? We are created in God's Image by God.'

We need to live to grow within our faults, enjoy ourselves, and enjoy the simple daily moments in life. Once we take time, even for twenty minutes alone daily, to understand ourselves, we will surely enjoy this life we live in.

"Only imagine Power"

Our thoughts are major forces that can build or destroy us.

'Now imagine this, who has control over our forces? Ourselves!'

We sometimes tend to say this person made me feel this way or that way; this is totally false; the only person that made you feel this way or that way is yourself.

'I/we forget that we give up control when we pass the blame over.'

When we keep control and learn to control how we feel, we remain in control. Life is beautiful when you take ownership and learn from one's shortcomings.

'Once our mindset shifts in the positive right direction, we grow.'

Always remember, sometimes we win, and sometimes we learn. Guys, we never lose if we learn. As you learn, get to laugh at yourself, you are human!

'What we focus on always grows. Focus on fear, and fear grows. Focus on faith, and faith grows.'

A true deep reflection within you will shed light unto your without.

'The biggest advantage is that we have the power to change ourselves within.'

In the same way, we can change what we grow in our garden, our within. We can clear, cut, and replant, and this will show up in our without.

'When fear takes the day.'

Guys, how come we allow fear to take the day? It gets worse when you seek advice from men of the cloth that are a lot of times filled with fear. For the most part, I personally find men of the cloth to be the most fearful of all yet they seek to give you words of advice that are usually filled with fear.

'The fearless are the go-getters, the entrepreneurs that set the blaze and change the world for the better.'

As entrepreneurs, we jump into the fire, feel the heat, feel the fear and yet still push forward.

'We create jobs for millions of people around the world, we improve our country's economy, and we are the Champions.'

Our Savior, Jesus Christ, was fearless, even when He was called shocking terrible names.

Jesus did feel fear towards his final days, but He faced His Fear with Faith.

2 Timothy: 1:7

"For God has not given you a spirit of fear & timidity, but of power, love, and self-discipline"

Based on those words, we can clearly see that our God demands we have courage.   It's important to balance who is giving you advice; even men of the cloth are giving advice filled with fear. This fear that they hold can pass onto you, for they are giving advice from areas they have no experience in.

'Jesus Christ was a risk-taker to the end and, in my eyes, the ultimate Entrepreneur.'

In this great journey called life, I continue to grow and learn from my successful failures.

'Guys, find it and build on it; your faith is already in you. Use it, and use your seed. Let it grow, take care of it, and feed it daily with positive thoughts.'

In turn, a positive thought attracts another positive thought.

"Go for it, follow your dreams actively, ignore the chickens, the noise makers, the ones going nowhere and fly high like the eagle and see you at the top!"

Jesus was called several derogatory names, and many groups of people walked away from Him. He was even called demon-possessed; this did not stop our Savior as He pushed on. He went forth and kept on delivering His message to His last Breath.

Remember this : *"When and only when you can see it, you can seize it."*

"The cause, not the effects"

We spend so much time focusing on the results and not the cause. The results are done and cannot be changed. Once we look over the cause, we learn from it and will be able to see the results. As we learn from each cause, we grow, and we enjoy the fact that we are human.

'Getting into the habit of being attentive will build us from the inside, and this is our within. In turn, from within ourselves will build our outside world'

Our God has already gifted us with all we will ever need. He has even guaranteed us in:

Jeremiah 29:13:

"When you seek Me, you will find Me. When you seek Me with all your heart."

The challenge comes back to us, did we really seek Him with all our hearts? Friends, keep investing in your greatest assets, that is, your mind and heart as you believe so it shall be. Keep these words close to your heart and spend Quite Quality time with yourselves daily. Seek Him Daily. He is waiting for you Daily.

'Winning is by Faith'

Never focus on the circumstances; these are only distractions. Keep your eyes on the goal, which is to keep the focus on your Faith.

'Keep pushing on the invisible on the unseen. How interesting is it that the most powerful experiences in life are from the invisible!'

We cannot see our Maker, we cannot see our Minds, nor our hearts, yet these form our very core, our within, and our strength. Friends, feeling fear is very okay. Once you feel the fear confirm so to yourself. Then connect to your Faith.

'Let's all: Feel the Fear and do it anyway.' This will grow you to always tap into the greatness that is inbuilt.'

It is during dark hours and nights when major changes and positive outcomes are taking place. Yes, it might not look like it or feel like it, but this is the game changer.

'The winning faith of the invisible.'

"The deep look."

The experienced deep look of growth comes into my eyes as I reflect on my successful failures. This look has the look of the eagle's eye; this deep look comes from one's soul.

'The painful heart bleeding experiences have taught me to always learn the lesson.'

This has taught me to keep at it, taught me to live, learn and grow.

'My pains have been and continue to be my gains.'

I have weathered the storms, the dark nights, the lonely nights, the ridicule, the insults, the embarrassments, the arrests, and the tears in my heart to come out on top.

'My scars have been and continue to be turned into stars.'

Friends, it has been tough, to say the least, but this has turned me into this great tested human being.

"I am not yet the Man I want to be, but I am sure not the Man I used to be."

I traveled the road less traveled and found my inner strength. Friends, it is already in you, in your within. As in the Word:

"Seek, and you will find, knock, and the door will be opened."

The issue at hand is we do not seek, we do not knock, yet we wait for the results. These are guarantees in the Bible. Do I really need to add anything more?

This is a tough one to say:

"Enjoy the failures and the pain, to enjoy the success and the gain."

Avoid everyone or anyone not on the same mission as you. This will grow your faith and push you to overcome your fears.

'In turn, the deep look of Victory will reflect in your eyes due to valuable growth experiences. '

"Dead on arrival ."

'Friends, no pain, no gain, and faith without action, are dead on arrival.'

These days, we seem to want the easy way out. We want to get our bodies in shape, but we don't want to do exercise. In turn, we look for shortcuts through, sometimes, liposuction. The exercise to achieve the same would have taken longer with a lot of pain. However, the end result with the exercise method would be a total, even balanced gain. The brain functions better, the heart functions better, the lungs function better, and you just feel and function better. The other option just has the fat cut out of you!

'The gain of Faith needs Pain and Action.'

These two go hand in hand, or else you are dead on arrival. This comment is used when a body comes into the hospital if the victim has passed away, "Dead on arrival." Successful businessmen know the pain with tears & persistence before we feel the sweet smell of success.

Over the last three decades of my successful failures, I have bled a lot, I have doubted a lot, I have cried a lot, and I have been insulted a lot. This has built me into a Great Victorious, Seasoned Entrepreneur. Boy, I'm totally ready to enjoy my gains!

'The bleeding tears of hurt and sorrow that streamed down my cheeks over the years have turned into tears of glory!'

"Victory is won by inches."

Friends, keep it simple; we just need to learn the lesson. When you learn the lesson, you have just turned your temporary failure into success.

'We are where we are today due to the decisions we made yesterday, good or bad.'

Going into a similar situation tomorrow, if you learned the lesson, the outcome will be different.

'Take ownership and avoid blame.'

Friends, you will be successful only when you take on ownership. We usually are quick to point fingers at others, to blame others; this is the most useless time ever wasted. Take a pause, take time to reflect, take time to learn, take time to smile, and grow from your experiences.

'A boxer wins the fight by throwing a punch the other opponent had not expected. A runner wins the race by a few inches to be declared world champion.'

In the business world, this only needs small daily steps forward.

'Smell and feel victory in your heart, and you will see victories.'

It is important to do your part, and God will surely do His part. Stop limiting God; we already have everything we need in life. The seed.

'Seeds have already been planted in you. I know for sure God will not do the planting.'

I find it shocking when I hear mature Christians say I am waiting on God. Waiting for what? You are just lazy and are trying to pass your laziness over to God. Now, friends, God is not lazy, and He detests laziness. So, pick yourselves up and get going, do your part!

"No honor in being poor"

I find it very perplexing how many Christians seem to think there is honor in being poor. They find refuge in using their faith as an excuse for being poor. This is mainly where Christians misuse the word patience.

'They actually do nothing as they claim to be waiting on God.'

We hear words like, 'In God's time' or 'when God allows.' Basically, one finds a place where they can blame God even after God has already gifted them. Yes, this is Blaming God as you claim to be waiting for God.

'God has done His part, so pick up and do your part using your God-given Gifts.'

As Christians, we can do more with more financial wealth to support ourselves and grow others.

Friends, there is no honor in being poor, and stop finding a reason or hiding behind your Fears.

'Don't talk about faith from your lips only but by your action in overcoming your Fear daily.'

If you are not using your God-given gifts, then stop always trying to find excuses.

'Another popular sentence I hear a lot is: "I am waiting for God to bless me." I hear this a lot. Imagine that God has blessed you and gifted you already, yet you are waiting! Rubbish!'

Being poor is your choice and hiding behind your Christianity is your excuse. What a waste of God-given talent, yet you allow fear to rule your day.

"Your oxygen mask on first"

Friends, in the plane before takeoff, we hear these few words:

"In the event of an emergency, the oxygen mask will drop; place yours on first before you place on others."

Yes, you first before you assist others, even your kids. The key reason for this is you must first take care of yourself, your family, and your business before assisting others. This is because the other way around, you might not even make it to assist others. The action of pulling and placing the mask on releases the flow of fresh oxygen into your body. It is only at this stage that one can assist others.

'In the same manner, the action of sorting yourself first is the only way you will have oxygen and strength in you to assist others.'

"Living by fear, not faith."

The older I get, the more I believe that the majority of people live in a fear-based society. We live with even men of the cloth advising us to live in fear and avoid taking risks. Our Savior was the ultimate risk-taker. So as the saying goes, "WWJD (What Would Jesus Do)," He would take the risk. Friends, to find your gifts take the risk. You will not only find your gifts but also use your gifts for glory.

'I can only imagine God looking down on us daily with a long sad face asking, 'When will you use your Gifts?''

The fear of the Lord is used by Christians in a negative light so many times. The fear of our Lord is having faith in our Lord.

'Fear turned to faith; faith the size of a mustard seed will give us glory.' Friends, go for it, take off the brakes and use your gifts.

"What is and Who is retarded?"

I can tell you, friends, that we tend to think   that people who are retarded are usually in hospitals. I have news for you. The majority of us face retardation and don't even know it.

'We get blinded by fear, pride, and arrogance.'

This causes us to live in a distorted world and not face reality. In my view, this is the definition of being retarded.

I dare to venture; we have a big percentage of politicians and religious leaders who have lost touch and don't know it. They are on autopilot and are retarded, moving around freely. In this case, both have lost touch with realities and have lost touch with our world. This is deeply sad for the blind are really leading the ones who need to be led.

'We sometimes run around seeking advice from retarded people that are free on our streets to offer advice with no substance at all.'

Friends, if you have ever seen one of the symptoms of a retarded person, it is like a lost person with no care or ownership. It's vital you take time to think of those around you, especially those placed in very key positions, before seeking advice.

"Losing touch"

How do we lose touch with reality? We live in our own world with open eyes, yet totally blinded. This has different effects on those who don't use their gifts; they switch to excuses. Then we have a different group of people, the fearful, who say, *"I am waiting for God. In the Bible, God asks us to be patient."* My dear friends, this does not mean that doing nothing is being patient. This group feels that they have found the best excuse where few will challenge them.

'They point the finger at the Bible and say it is in the Bible as one of the virtues of the Holy Spirit.'

What a cheap excuse due to their own fear.

'One must find the pulse, the strength, and the energy to keep at it.'

In the Word, we are told to knock, and the door will be opened. How can you sit back, relax and do nothing?

'We will get the change that we seek.'

In the Word, it says seek, and you will find. I tell you; it is impossible to expect change when you do not change.

'Patience means to keep at it daily with simple small positive steps forward.' Take time to look over daily what is working for you and what is not working for your benefit. Then drop the bad habits and reinforce the good habits. Open your eyes and your heart daily during your precious quiet times.

'It's only during this time your mind, heart, and soul are all connected as one.'

"Bricks for?"

As I look back over the years of my last decade, my forties, I ponder on all the bricks thrown at me with lies, insults, and false claims. I was tried and tested. The bricks thrown at me were to destroy me. Friends, these very bricks have built me into a better, stronger, and deeper person. The bricks have supported me in building my solid foundation.

'Due to all these bricks thrown at me, I was able to rebuild my house with God at the center.'

I am able to smile from the pain of rejection and insults. All of my material possessions were stolen from me in Rwanda. However, I can still look my enemies in the eyes and say, *"I forgive you."*

'The haters have remained, and some have disappeared, but their injections of venom no longer sting in my life.'

As one of the songs goes… *"It's going to be a Bright, bright, bright sunny day…."*

'Friends, do not let haters define who you are.'

Be who God created you to be, as these same haters have not found their purpose in life. In turn, they want you to lose your God-given Purpose.

"Defeated Frenemies "

I watch the anger and bitterness rot away in the eyes of my former friends as they continue to see God's Victories in my life. The depth of anger comes from the fact I did not follow their ill advice over the last two decades. Friends, this is advice from frenemies that also involve family members, sadly enough. This is clearly covered in the word, the

Bible. *"Oh, the joys of those who do not follow the advice of the wicked…."*

These fake members of family and friends are heading nowhere and would like you to join them on their nowhere journey. Oh God, I thank You for watching over me and looking ahead behind the bend for me.

<u>Thought to Self:</u>

I find it so preflexing at the turn of a new year; we get to hear the same words over and over again; this is your year of change. We even get to hear the same from Fathers and Men of the Cloth. This is your year; all is going to change.

As I have always said: "Change will Only Happen When We Change from Within and Stop Finding Excuses and Stop Blaming God ."

This is another feather in my hat and yet another one of my steps within the thousand steps since our Savior, Jesus Christ, was never a coward. Why should you or I be a coward? Be brave, go for it, and use your God-given Gifts. Let's meet at the top!

Successful Failures Lesson Take Away:

'I thank You, Lord, for giving me the wisdom and insight to see tomorrow today. It feels great; I feel lighter; I feel joyful and at total peace, for I was also a Father to my kids during their formative years.'

This is yet another feather on my hat of victory, victory, and victory! I learned yet another lesson of trust and dependence on My God Alone.

This has been yet another successful failure. Finding and searching for you from within and not from without. In the end, you must be you and only you.

Chapter 13 - The Lord is my Shepard

Description: Psalm 23

In God's Hands

'I have learned to grow by letting go in order to grow and find peace. When one's heart is at Peace sets the fertile soil for balanced growth.'

The stinging pain of betrayal as loved ones and friends become your enemies. My ex-wife Cleophase and my ex-friends turned on me, over a decade ago, and became my enemies with hate in their hearts. This pain sits deep into one's core. It's like pulling your flesh apart and watching blood drip through your muscles.

'I Do turned into I Don't.'

The same lady I said 'I Do' to in 2002, 'with words of through richer or poor,' had turned into my Foe. The finger was pointed at me by my wife, then Cleophase Kabasiita. She sidestepped me and watched the wolves come for my blood. It was so heartbreaking when I look back through my forties on her efforts to try and support having me destroyed. The woman, my former wife, that slept beside me for a decade had turned into my biggest critic. She watched from the sidelines as she flamed the fires to try and have me arrested and eliminated. It was beyond heartbreaking to see those precious marital words before God meant nothing at all to Cleophase.

'The strength within comes from forgiveness and letting go.'

Friends, it's not easy, but this is your life. Do not let outside forces control your inside life. We are in God's Hands.

"False belief"

On the Christian side of life, some people tend to think that Jesus's mission was to come to judge. This train of thought is off.

'Our Savior Jesus Christ came to Love, and through this most powerful Love, we have a transformation of the heart.'

Sadly, I witness so many Christians quick to sit on the high stool to pass judgment. If our Savior Jesus Christ did not come to judge, how dare we judge? I marvel in surprise as I listen to so many Christians passing judgment over other fellow brothers and sisters.

"The Power of Love is what we all need to focus on."

We can serve God, not in the old way of obeying the letter of the Law, but in the new way of living in the Spirit.

How?

'Through loving friends, not through judging each other day in and day out.'

"Laziness in Faith"

It's sad to say this, but it is true to say this: 'I have seen too many Christians find comfort through their laziness in Faith'

I have watched and continue to watch friends and family find a shield of protection through their laziness in faith.

Keywords used by my fellow Christians:

> "I am waiting for God's time"

> "When God opens the door for me"

> "It's God's decision."

OR

"I am waiting for God to open the right door."

"I will wait for God's perfect timing, He knows best."

Another one: "Don't you know that one of the virtues of the Holy Spirit is patience." My Fellow Christians give themselves comfort and say they are waiting on God. This is their best excuse for their failures of not even trying to make their life better here on earth.

"What's the reason for this laziness in Faith?"

The reason is these people have found, so they think, the perfect excuse, blame God.

'Once you blame God, no one tries to question you. Since, you are sitting back, waiting for God to open the door for you. Let's keep in mind God has already done His Part when we created you.'

Instead of using your God-given gifts, you try to hide them and deep-down blame God; how Sad.

In this way, you stay in your comfort zone, waiting for God to act and a lot of people will not question your waiting and doing nothing.

'Did you know the word hands in the Bible means for action.?'

'Go forth, and use your good God-given gifts to make this world a better place. There is great beauty and great joy once you search for your Gifts and use them daily.'

'His Image Power Within.'

Friends, God created us in His image. Do you know what this means? He has given us the power to go forth and seize our dreams with active action.

Behind these comments, this group feel they are just following the Bible and misusing the word Patience to mean doing nothing. What a waste of our God God-given Human Gifts and Talents. Yet, most of this group of people are quick to point out the mistakes made as they sit on the sidelines of life. *'They have found their safe zone with what looks like the perfect hideout, laziness in faith.'*

This laziness in Faith means they are actually pushing the blame on God.

'Where is the honor' ?

Friends, where is the honor of thinking and acting poor that I see so many Christian Brothers and Sisters showing off? I listen as the different voices portray a sense of self-pride and comfort in being poor. It's like one feels being poor brings one closer to God. In other words, do not use your God-given Gifts as you play life safe due to allowing fear to overcome your faith. Then after months and years of doing so, you remain poor and added to that, you remain comfortable. This is not honorable at all in any way.

We all go through stages of being broke; this is okay and usually temporary. *'The stage of being broke is temporary as long as you are working on solutions to pull out.'*

'The real danger is being poor. It's very simple to test if you are poor.'

To be poor is a mindset with a focus on blaming someone else. I am poor because this and that was done to be or done to my family. Once you blame someone else for your current position in life, you have given up control over to the other person.

The reason behind this blame game is to try and give one comfort; it's not one's fault.

'When one hides behind another person blocking them, it gives one a false sense of a comfort zone.'

A place to hide and try and feel better about one's self. It's through this blame game that the finger is pointed to someone else as the reason why they are poor.

Our Savior was not poor in any way, shape, or form. He changed our world forever through using His Gifts here on earth. Sadly, I see so many Christian Brothers and Sisters claiming they could not achieve their desired goals because they are poor. We each came into this earth with our own unique God-given gifts.

'Those who have not used their God-given gifts cannot claim any honor.'

If you are poor in mind you will be poor on earth.

'There is no honor in being poor at all. Friends, if you think there is honor, you must be joking!'

There is nothing wrong with being rich, in being wealthy, when you use your riches for doing good. The rich person uses his gifts to better his life, his family's life, and those around him and beyond. This does not compare to the poor person who never does anything but complain and blame others. In our Good Book:

Psalm 62:10 "Don't make your living by extortion or put your hope in stealing. And if your wealth increases, don't make it the center of your life."

"Caution: Wet floor."

During one of the services at Nairobi Chapel in 2018, the Pastor talked about the networks we have in life. His focus in this service touched on the level of one aspect of the business as he watered down the no need to focus on tenders or networks in business or life. The Pastor made it sound like focusing on getting tenders is a bad thing. The other comment he made was it's not about our networks that are important.

'Totally Opposite: Our Savior was all about getting the right networks and the right disciples.'

It's this kind of advice that I totally differ from the Pastor's as his advice comes from a place of no experience at all. This is the kind of advice I refer to as, 'Caution Wet Floor.'

As Pastors themselves get their own jobs through networks all the time. This is a solid case of a Pastor leading this flock on this day in the wrong direction. The sad part would be those young minds that took his advice on this day.

'Advice that carries no value at all and the total opposite advice that adds no value at all.'

It is through getting the right tender, in the right way, with God always at the center, that one creates employment. In turn, thousands of families have food on their tables to eat for weeks, months, and sometimes years on end. This is the kind of unbalanced advice that has no depth of connection that holds back those that seek his advice.

The very same Pastor gets a job based on his connections. There is nothing wrong with having the right connections or winning any rightful tenders. It's these people who believe and use their connections and tenders to better their lives and enrich their lives.

'It's these people that change the world along the way and make this world a better place to live in. I am grateful I am one of them.'

Let's dive deeper in with an additional comment which the Pastor said to wait for God's timing. Friends, this comment has turned many people/believers into simply lazy. It's sickening, to say the least, when I hear people say, 'I am waiting on God.'   What a so-called perfect excuse! It's now because of God that you sit back and hide behind Him, waiting. Yes, one of the virtues of the Holy Spirit is patience. This does not mean you sit back and become lazy using our Savior as your excuse.

I find this very sad and see this laziness mindset taking center stage with so many Pastors and many family members.

Thoughts to Self:

Friends, 'Caution: Wet floor.' This is yet again one of my successful failures to have a clear discernment and weed out the weeds.

***

"My past molded me to be better and not bitter; this is why I shine in God's Victories".

"Born again."

We use these words a lot as Christians, *'I am born again.'*

When we do so as we refer to the spirit of new life born again, we say and claim we are newly born in the Spirit.   I, too, am born again and was born again in the Spirit on December 30, 2011.

'It is the greatest super great feeling to be a new being coming alive with the Spirit in me.'

As I look deeper into my fellow Christian brothers and sisters who are born again, I wonder if they are born again in mind. Have their minds shifted from dreamers to dreamers that are doers also? I have noticed a change in Spirit for the better within my fellow Christian Brothers and Sisters once they have given their lives to Jesus.

'The sad part is their mindset stays the same.'

I hear their powerful earth-shaking Prayers go on and on for months on end.

'The lacking part that remains is that there is, No action behind their Prayers at all.'

The reasoning continues, 'patience' is one of the virtues of the Holy Spirit. This group of people will state: *I am in this current position because God told me to wait.* I really fail to understand how our Father in Heaven wants one to sit back and wait in Laziness for HIM, our God. The true reality is that one has found comfort in blaming God .

'To be really "Born Again," must involve the Mind and Spirit together as One.'

Our minds must be "Born Again" this means born fresh if we want our world to change. I have witnessed a lot of Christians that are quick with words of faith. However, they show signs of living by fear and not by Faith.

'In my opinion, to be really "Born Again," a new Believer needs to be a doer also.'

A person of action behind one's Prayers. In life, you will get knocked down; You will be called names; you will be insulted and go through a lot of hardships along your active journey of Life. Reach out, fight for your dreams, and walk the path alone sometimes.

Psalm 23."

My successful failures are not failures when I learn the lesson behind each failure.

As I sit here again in my beautiful garden at home with the morning breeze on my cheeks, I listen to the morning birds telling each other their morning stories.

'I am reminded in my thoughts of the life I have lived. The challenges I have gone through, and the enemies I have overcome.'

The light bulb in my mind switches on to **Psalm 23**.

"*The Lord is my Shepherd. I have all that I need. He lets me rest in green meadows; He leads me beside peaceful streams. He renews my strength. He guides me along the right paths, bringing honor to His name. Even when I walk through the darkest valley, I will not be afraid, for you are close beside me; your rod and Your staff protect and comfort me. You prepare a feast for me in the presence of my enemies. You honor me by anointing my head with oil. My cup overflows with blessings. Surely, your goodness and unfailing love will pursue me all the days of my life, and I will live in the house of the Lord forever."*

At the end of the day, my life has been filled with victories. This mainly comes from who you turn to when you feel down and out. In my case, I turned to God. No matter what you go through, if you learn the lesson, you will come out on top.

'The sweet smell of victory as I grow daily gives me great Peace.'

In Peace, we find our core, and we grow and build our lives for the better daily. Once you seek and search for Peace, everything else comes in line.

'World Seasoned Three Decades.'

As a global seasoned entrepreneur I have kept at it with all efforts & I keep going forward daily. Yes, mistakes I have made & keep making different mistakes. Key here is the valuable growth lesson. The good that has come from my many different business ventures has changed and improved thousands of lives around the world.

'I came to know in my heart that I have changed the world to make it better for thousands of people.'

On the other hand, the non-doers get to hear of my mistakes from time to time. This is when they become active to jump up and point at my mistakes. **'This is where the non-doers spend their time waiting for the Hero to make a mistake.'**

Really what advice would I get from a non-doer ? Really think about it.

'Its through changing the world, its through making mistakes, that I have done my part in making this world a better place. I have left my positive mark in this world of ours.'

Thoughts to Self:

***

"I came, I saw and I conquered"

"God's power has and continues to leave my enemies and frenemies in shock"

"The way forward matters more than where you are coming from."

"Talk to your problems about how big your God is."

Successful Failures Lesson Take Away:

'In the end, you will feel the test of God's sweet victory. Friends, show God your Faith, not your fear. In fear, we have little or no faith.

'When you swing your sword out, it gets God's attention, for this is Prayer with action .

'I have pulled out my sword many times, over the last twelve years, and so can you.'

Printed in the USA
CPSIA information can be obtained
at www.ICGtesting.com
LVHW051437180224
772154LV00009B/103